A War on the Wards
1939-1945

J Crozier

Pen Press Publishers Ltd

First published in Great Britain by
Pen Press Publishers Ltd
25 Eastern Place
Brighton
BN2 1GJ

ISBN 978-1-906206-30-7

Printed and bound in the UK

A catalogue record of this book is available from
the British Library

Cover design by Jacqueline Abromeit

About the Author

Having spent most of the war years confined to life in Sanatoria, the author had some difficulty in obtaining suitable employment following cessation of hostilities.

Finally, he accepted a position of site-clerk with a large building company, with contractors all over Scotland, and for the next thirty-five years continued in administration work with another two companies in the construction industry, culminating in a position of company secretary with a small, successful and profitable specialist civil engineering contractor, which was taken over by a large English contractors consortium, resulting in 're-organisation' and subsequent redundancy at the age of 59.

Again, being unsuccessful in obtaining suitable employment this time at such an age, he emigrated to Spain, where for a few years in semi-retirement he undertook duties as a part-time accountant with an English property agency, before returning to the new town of East Kilbride where he now lives, aged 85.

CONTENTS

PROLOGUE

It is possible for someone to contract tuberculosis and not show any symptoms for years after exposure.

Symptoms include prolonged cough, weight loss, poor appetite, high temperature, lassitude or excessive sweating, particularly at night.

To all those of my acquaintance who were afflicted by, and subsequently succumbed to this devastating disease, this true story is dedicated.

INTRODUCTION

My Wartime Experience and How I Fought *A War on the Wards*

EXPERIENCE: One dictionary definition given for war is 'to fight or battle' and as this narrative unfolds it will amply describe my own personal battle against a life-threatening disease in my earlier years.

During the war of 1939-45 we, all of my age group, had experiences of some sort or another, but mine may be somewhat different to any other, and may even be unique.

As we are all now aware, everyone in the nation had to contribute in some measure, however small, to the national war effort, by falling into one of the following categories, for example:

Serving in the forces, including the Merchant Navy etc – I was not in this category!

Reserved occupations – for those who had 'special knowledge and experience' to promote the war effort on the 'home front' – I was not in this group!

Essential Works Order – where men (and women) were directed into employment in various industries and other activities to supply goods and services to augment the war effort – I was not in this directive!

I was not a conscientious objector!

I was not interned as a foreign national, who may hinder the war effort!

I was not in prison!

I was not mentally or physically disabled and was in possession of all my senses of hearing, sight, touch, smell and taste.

I lived legally, and never moved outwith the West of Scotland area.

So what did I do to contribute in playing a part, however small, during the six years of conflict, in what many consider to be the country's gravest hour of need?

I did nothing!

Let me explain.

CHAPTER 1

Call-Up

I celebrated my 17th birthday on 2nd September 1939 and the following morning at 11am the family huddled around the 'wireless' to hear an announcement by the Prime Minister, Neville Chamberlain, who informed us that as no response had been received from Germany to our ultimatum to cease aggression in Poland, the country was now at war.

We then knew that mobilisation orders would soon be issued, and all members of the male population between the ages of 18-35 would be liable for 'call-up'. Within a few weeks, my brother was inducted to the army and after training was sent to India, where he spent the rest of the war. Under the Essential Works Order, my sister was sent to a factory in Wishaw, where she worked long hours until the tide of war turned in our favour and then returned to normal working hours.

Meantime, I was employed as a junior clerk in an engineering works in Hamilton, which I had joined after leaving school. My duties, as part of a team, were to record orders from receipt through manufacture, assembly, despatch and final billing. I enjoyed my work, and seemed to have gained the confidence of my senior colleagues. My working hours were 9am till 5pm Monday to Friday, but as other members of staff left for the forces, these were changed to 7.30am till 5pm Monday till Friday, with Saturdays from 8am till 12.30pm, and with overtime on Tuesdays and Thursdays and also occasionally on Sundays. So my workload increased as time went on and I knew that in about a year's time, I too would be leaving.

The 'brown envelope' duly arrived shortly after my 18th birthday in 1940, informing me to attend Mason Street Motherwell recruiting office for assessment and medical examination. When I arrived there, a large number of men were being prepared for induction and after giving personal details so that we were classified as being 'suitable square pegs to be fitted into round holes', as was the accepted practice, we were taken to another room for medical examination. This consisted of an eye and hearing test and a dental examination; we were also checked for flat feet and any missing or partial limbs. Our chests were examined by stethoscope and we were asked to cough. At this point, I was asked to stand aside, as the examining doctor said he needed a second opinion, which I finally got as I was last in the queue. The doctor then informed me that he would write to the medical officer for health for Hamilton, who would then contact me by letter.

I returned to work.

A few weeks later I received a letter from Dr Gilmour, the medical officer, instructing me to attend Strathclyde Hospital in Motherwell for a medical examination. This would consist of a chest X-ray only, the result of which would be passed to Dr Gilmour, who would then communicate with me further.

I returned to work.

CHAPTER 2

A Bolt from the Blue

A few weeks later I received a letter from Dr Gilmour inviting me to his office for a further examination. During this meeting he gave me the 'good news/bad news' syndrome. The good news (according to him) was that I was grade 4F and unfit for service in the forces – the bad news was that I had the worst combination of any two letters in the alphabet – TB! I was absolutely shattered! I could not understand – I was feeling fit – I played amateur football (not very well) and was a member of Hamilton Cycling Club covering many miles on Sundays.

The only knowledge I had of tuberculosis was that it was an illness to which people succumbed quite quickly. However, he hastened to assure me this was not the case, as treatment was available, and he would arrange this as soon as possible, although it would take some time and hospitalisation could take up to nine months or so. He then informed me that I could not mix in crowds, such as cinema, theatre, football matches or dancing, and to avoid travelling on crowded buses or trains, as TB was highly contagious. I should also cover my mouth with a handkerchief when coughing. He then gave me a dark blue coloured bottle, with a black screw cap – this to expectorate into and flush the contents down the toilet. He said I could return to work, giving me a sick note for one week, but that he would write to my employer, asking them to arrange for a shorter working week and that, whenever possible, I should walk to and from work and not travel by bus.

When I returned to work, the office manager informed me that my duties were changed and that I would be in an office on my own which had been a reception room. The furniture of this new office consisted of a double pedestal wooden desk with an ink-well, blotting pad, pen, pencil, ruler and a hard cover handy reckoner for calculations as I would now be responsible for wages, purchase and sales ledgers.

My new hours would be from 10am till 4pm with no Saturdays or Sundays and each day's work would be left out for me each morning and should be left by me each afternoon for placing in the office safe until use the following day. This meant being isolated from the other members of staff – no chance of me spreading any germs!

As I looked from my window, I saw opposite two propaganda signs on the billboards opposite – the first one said 'Be like Dad – Keep Mum' and the other (which was obviously directed at me) read 'Coughs and Sneezes Spread Diseases'.

I then settled into a routine of walking to and from work and my evenings were spent reading library books, listening to the radio and playing dominoes and cards with my parents – dominoes always being won by Father and cards by Mother (who was a bit of a card-sharp!) On Saturdays and Sundays I would leave home about 10 am with sandwiches from what was available from the rations and a small bottle of milk, returning at about tea-time, having spent the day walking around all the country roads in the Hamilton area. On one occasion, I walked to Loudoun Hill near Darvel in Ayrshire, a total distance of approximately 35 miles, returning home at about 7pm.

I very rarely saw any of my friends, as they spent their leisure time in activities which were banned to me, so I walked hundreds of miles every week, and in doing so wore out a number of pairs of shoes – using precious clothing coupons!

I had become, literally, a RECLUSE!

It was now 1941.

CHAPTER 3

An Introduction to 'The San'

In due course, I received a letter from Dr Gilmour, medical officer for health for the Hamilton area informing me that he had, at last, obtained a place for me at Bridge of Weir Sanatorium and I should report there at 1 pm on a certain date. A list of items to be taken was also enclosed and so I packed the following items in my case – change of clothing, including underwear, slippers, toothbrush, dentifrice (SR type), shaving equipment, identity card, ration book and gas mask (still in cardboard box and unused). As I did not have a dressing gown, my father gave me his and as he was the same height as me, it fitted perfectly.

Accompanied by my mother, we travelled by train from Hamilton to Glasgow, thence to Bridge of Weir where a small local bus connected with the train service taking us to the main gate of the sanatorium. There were another eight or so passengers and most got off with us and I realised, as they were all women, they must be members of staff.

As we left the bus, I looked down the valley and got my first view of what was to be my 'home' for several months ahead. It consisted of a long red stone building with three blocks of ground floor passages and two storeys connected by another two fairly long ground floor passages or 'solaria'. We approached the first door marked 'Pavilion 1' only to be told to go to Pavilion 3 as the first two were for female patients and number 3 was for men.

As we approached Pavilion 3, I saw the inscription in stone above the door, which said 'Come unto me all ye that labour and are heavy laden and I will give you rest'.

The sanatorium was part of the Quarriers' village homes complex, which was quite extensive. It consisted of the cottages themselves as well as a unit for physically disabled children, a unit for mentally handicapped people, an epileptic 'colony' and workshops. There was also a small farm which cultivated grounds for vegetables and plants, the produce from which supplemented the national ration allowance.

I pressed the door bell which was answered by a nurse, smartly dressed in blue check uniform with brilliant white starched cuffs, belt and collar and white nurse's cap. She invited us to enter and led us down a corridor of terrazzo type flooring to a heavy panelled timber door with ornate framing and a brass doorknob, highly polished. The door was marked 'Duty Room'. She knocked and a voice from within called "Come." We entered – to be met by a nurse dressed in uniform similar to 'our' nurse but in a dark blue colour and her cap was tied under her chin by a blue ribbon. She was seated at a desk with another nurse dressed in a royal blue uniform standing beside her.

The formal welcome and introductions were made, but she immediately entered into a discourse of what I could expect during my stay and what would be expected of me. She said that I would receive the best of care and attention by a devoted and dedicated staff and would be treated at all times with courtesy, which I should reciprocate in similar fashion.

Discipline and punctuality were the key watchwords, as at certain times of the day things would happen and it was essential that punctuality be observed to enable the hospital to function properly. A strict code of conduct prevailed which I must maintain at all times and I was also to be neat and tidy in my attire and general appearance.

I was to address the staff by their proper rank and be willing to assist them in any light duties that I may be asked to undertake. A rule of no smoking and no drinking of alcohol was strictly in force and non-observance could lead to instant discharge. I was not to have any communication with any patients in Pavilions 1 and 2 (the women's pavilions) and was to stay within the perimeter of the hospital grounds. If I were to observe all these conditions, then peace and harmony would prevail and I would leave in better health and mind at the end of my stay. She then rose from her chair saying, "I will now leave you in the hands of Sister Simpson," and with that, she swept from the room.

Sister Simpson was a person in her mid-30s and reasonably tall in stature. She seemed to have a much better disposition and, as I was later to realise, was a strict but fair disciplinarian but without whom my hospital stay would not have been so bearable. She reiterated the points made by matron regarding the hospital regime and how discipline was foremost in achieving success in my treatment. After detailing the routine to which I would be subjected, she said that in future, if I had any problems, difficulties or required any advice, I must discuss the matter with her only and no other member of staff – whether doctors, nurses, auxiliaries or maids – and the matter would be resolved without any 'tittle tattle' which could, perhaps, disturb the peace and harmony of the system.

As I later discovered, Sister Simpson was respected by all – patients, doctors, nurses, maids and even visitors. In my humble opinion, she should have been in the honours list! She told Mother that the visiting hours were 2pm till 4pm on Saturdays and that at 2pm the main door would be opened and at 3.50pm a bell would be rung to allow visitors to vacate the building by 4pm prompt, when the main door would again be secured. She concluded her talk by again confirming that if I abided by all the conditions, there would be no problems and she looked forward to a suitable nurse/patient relationship. She shook hands with Mother then rang a small hand bell on the desk and when a nurse entered she said, "Take Crozier to his allotted bed and see him properly inducted." I went to lift my case, but Sister said, "Maid Hamilton will carry your case," and together we ascended the two flights of stairs leading to the top floor.

Arriving at the top floor, we were in front of a heavy panelled timber door, beautifully polished, with similar timber ornate frames and held open by a wooden wedge. As we entered the room, I noticed that the floor was also highly polished and the walls were painted dark green. Being an old building the ceiling was high, with tall windows, the panes of which were painted black and taped to comply with blackout regulations. The lower sashes were raised to allow light (and fresh air) in and I was later made acquainted with the procedures to enable the blackout regulations to be observed. The lower sashes were lowered by the maids when darkness approached. This was done by wooden poles fitted with hooks and the lights were then switched on. At about 8pm (which was 'lights out' time) they would reverse the procedure and the room would be in darkness and open to the elements – fresh air, wind, rain and even snow! In the morning, the procedure would again be reversed.

There were eight beds in the room and I had been allocated the second bed on the right, near the door. In diagonal corners were two large wooden wardrobes to contain all eight patients' belongings. My bed was of metal construction with a coiled spring mattress, solid legs (no wheels, as fitted to modern hospital beds) and the same height as the other seven (no adjustment, as found on modern hospital beds). There was a solid wooden bedside cabinet on top of which was a glass of water and a white enamel mug with a blue rim and flip top. This was a sputum mug with a sticky tape label with my name on it. There was also a pair of earphones draped over the back of the bed to listen to the BBC Home Service and the hospital's own record programme. In the centre of the room there was a solid wooden table and four straight-backed chairs.

The nurse then brought over a set of screens of brilliant white colour and placed them round the bed (no overhead rails or patterned curtains as today) and told me to undress and put on my pyjamas, slippers and dressing gown and then lie on top of the bed. The screens were then removed and my clothes (including my 'Attaboy' hat – remember the slogan – 'If you want to get ahead get a hat') were taken by the maid and placed in the nearer wardrobe. The nurse then asked my mother to leave, reminding her of the visiting times on Saturdays.

As I looked around me, I noticed that some patients were dressed, lying on top of their beds, whilst others were under the sheets. There was total silence and nobody seemed to speak, although some were listening on their earphones. The reason for the silence and inactivity was that this was a rest period and it was later explained to me that there were two such periods daily (between 10-11am and 2-3pm) when the whole place literally shut down – and when the silence was absolutely deafening! A few minutes later a bell rang indicating the end of the rest hour and some activity took place with some patients getting up and moving about whilst others stayed in bed – this was because some patients were considered to be in better health than others.

The chap in the next bed then got up and introduced himself as Jackie Overend from Rutherglen. He was about 30 years old with fair hair and turned out to be a good companion. He said that I would no doubt find things to be rather strange, but I would soon get used to the routine and that as long as I followed the rules I would 'get by' all right. I told him I had been told I would be in for about 9 months and that I hoped things would go well. He replied, "I should not place too much reliance on what they tell you and whilst I am not trying to discourage or disappoint you, very few go out of here in that time, and those that do are usually in a wooden box. Don't put too much faith in the inscription above the entrance as most of the patients here translate that as 'Abandon hope, all ye who enter'."

What an encouraging welcome to my new 'home'. I was absolutely shaken by what he had just said and asked him when he was likely to go home. He replied that he was on the basic treatment of fresh air and rest only. I then asked him how long he had been here and he replied, "Seventeen months this time." THIS TIME! He must have been here before and on mentioning this he replied that the last time was before the start of the war and he had been in for 19 months then. I made a quick calculation – 17 plus 19 months equals three years! My God, it was like a prison sentence – and in some respects it was!

Jackie then said he would show me where the bathroom was located and took me along the corridor to where it was situated. The room consisted of six wash-hand basins, four toilet cubicles and a bathroom. On seeing this I said that I might take a bath soon to which he replied, "No way! You will be told when to take a bath – this is to ensure everyone has a supervised bath on a regular basis and that the use of hot water is controlled." We then returned to the ward where we sat down at the table and he gave me his daily newspaper, informing me that this could be bought from the paper boy (who was actually a 60-year-old patient named Haggerty) – but no papers on the Sabbath!

I then asked Jackie how one could pass the time of day and he replied that he wrote short stories in the hope of publication but to date with no success. (I later learned that he had the greatest number of rejection slips but had some success later). He then gave me a book to read, advising me that I should arrange for my visitors to bring me two books from Hamilton library, read one and return it for another each week and so on, and this would give me an interest as the atmosphere could be quite soul destroying after a while. He said that this would help keep my spirits up as in his opinion more patients died of the three Ds (depression, despondency and despair) than ever actually died of TB.

I then asked him about the food; he replied it was quite good, although no one asked for 'seconds'. He told me that as TB was a wasting and debilitating disease, there were no obese or even fat people there. It was then I realised that the few people I had seen so far were, indeed, quite thin and some even appeared gaunt and on reflection, I felt that I too was slim, being 6ft tall and weighing under nine stones. (I haven't changed much in 60 years – I am still 6ft tall).

After tea at the table, the blackout procedure took place and after supper of hot milk, tea or cocoa, the lights were put out at 8 o'clock. From the dull, sombre atmosphere of the place, added to the apparent feeling of hopelessness and the information given to me by Jackie, I felt I was already a candidate for the three Ds. As a result I had a most unpleasant and restless night.

With the dawn comes another day, but would it be any

more hopeful and cheerful than the previous 24 hours? I had my breakfast of porridge, scrambled, powdered egg, toast and tea at the table alone, as some of the others had gone to the main dining hall. Jackie had told me to stay in the ward and not to wander about, so that the staff would know where I was. About 9 o'clock, old Haggerty the paper boy arrived and when I told him I had no money with me he agreed to supply me with daily papers for the rest of the week and for me to pay him on Monday after my visitors had seen me on Saturday. About 9.30am the nurse came and said she would take me to the Duty Room where Sister took a blood test and asked me how I was settling in. I decided not to tell her how I really felt, but replied, "Fine," (which I don't think she believed). She then asked me to bring down my ration book that the hospital would keep during my stay.

I went along the corridor to the stairs and started to climb these two at a time, as I felt strong enough to do so. Then I heard a voice call, "STOP." I stopped, to be confronted by a nurse, aged about 40-ish, with grey hair and dressed in a slightly different uniform to the other nurses. She said to me in a soft voice, "You're a new boy here?"

I replied, "Yes."

"Then let me inform you that no one rushes around in this hospital, not even in emergencies – nurses may use hurried steps, but no one runs – understood?" I nodded my agreement. "From now on you will walk steadily at San pace. Now carry on." I carried on at 'San' pace.

I mentioned my encounter to Jackie, who replied, "That would be Staff Nurse Cameron – actually she's OK."

I then asked, "What is 'San' pace?"

"That is the expression used to denote the pace used in walking in a sanatorium – you'll get used to it – like everything else here."

And to this day I still walk at San pace! I also discovered

that everything connected with the hospital was always referred to as 'the San'.

For the next fortnight or so, I was confined to the ward and spent the time reading the daily paper and library books and listening to the record request programme. This was broadcast between 9-10am and 6-7pm on Mondays to Fridays from the radio room situated at the end of the corridor from the ward.

Occasionally, I looked out of the windows and saw below a sward of green lawn that was well maintained with shrubs, rhododendron bushes and lined with trimmed edge footpaths covered in reddish chips – but I never saw anyone! I had always considered myself to be a cheery, optimistic individual, but at the end of this period, the heavy air of resignation, the lack of any atmosphere of comradeship with very little conversation was beginning to affect me and although I felt good physically, I did feel like a likely candidate for the three Ds mentally.

So I decided to take up Sister's original offer of friendly consideration of any arising problems but was pre-empted in this respect, because, by sheer coincidence, the following morning during her round of inspection, she notified me that I was being moved to a room on the ground floor. There I was to undergo a course of medication designed at improving my general health preparatory to starting a full operational course of treatment later. My despondency evaporated into thin air and I felt quite buoyed up by the prospect of new surroundings.

Later that day I said farewell to Jackie and my cell(?) room mates and being led by a nurse, with me carrying my glass of water in one hand and my sputum mug in the other, followed by the maid carrying my suitcase, we all descended the two flights of stairs to the ground floor.

CHAPTER 4

New Horizons

As we walked along the corridor on the ground floor, I noticed two or three rooms with wood-panelled doors, wedged open, and at the end of the corridor I entered a similar type of room. The first thing I noticed was that the walls were painted yellow, with a window, framed by heavy material curtains, again to comply with blackout regulations. The window panes, however, were not painted black and did not have any black paper taped on them, but instead offered an uninterrupted view of the grounds, which I had seen from my first-floor room (nicknamed the 'Monkey Run' – don't ask me why because nobody seemed to know). The room that I had now entered was called the 'Sun Room' as it faced south and was bathed in sunshine for most of the day during good weather. The ceiling of the room was much lower than the previous room and the size of the windows smaller, but still with the bottom sashes raised to allow the fresh air in – the main treatment for TB!

There were two beds, a wooden wardrobe and a small table with the customary cabinets beside the beds. I was allocated a bed further from the window, whilst the other bed was occupied by a man in his 30s named Jim Russell. The usual introductions were made and I was then told by the nurse that, until further notice, I would be confined to bed – my optimism suddenly began to disappear at this news but I took the philosophical view that if this was going to help me in my fight against this awful disease, then so be it.

I was later to realise how lucky I was, having been moved to this particular room, because Jim turned out to be a most congenial and encouraging roommate. He had a most influential bearing on my future approach and outlook for the remainder of my stay in the San, which would eventually lead to a longer life expectancy than I ever believed possible at that particular moment. Jim had been a senior executive in one of the departments in Glasgow Corporation and was very knowledgeable in most subjects. He possessed a sharp wit and being a good conversationalist, he always kept my spirits up if I ever felt down. His pearls of wisdom and encouragement helped me beyond measure. We spent our days in conversations on various subjects and topics, reading books and newspapers and doing jigsaws and crosswords. Jim introduced me to the game of 'battleships', starting off with small grids and working up to very large ones. On one occasion the game lasted two days before a victory. We also listened to the BBC Home Service programmes, including morning and afternoon sessions of *Music While You Work* – although we did no work!

We also listened to the daily record request programmes from the San's own radio room and which bored us to tears (almost) listening to the presenter (whom I never met). He introduced the records in a dull monotonous voice with the following examples: "The next record is Richard Tauber singing *Because*…The next record is the Boston Symphony Orchestra playing *The Blue Danube Waltz*…The next record is Bing Crosby singing *Blue Skies*…" and so on until one day

I said to Jim, "I'm going to beat this horrible disease and as soon as I am fit enough, I'm going to take over this programme and brighten and cheer up the whole place," –little realising at that time just what an impact such a situation was going to have on the whole atmosphere within the San's routine. Jim's reply was, "Good lad – go for it – you can do it!" My well-being then rose dramatically!

Ninety-nine percent of the patients suffered from pulmonary TB but Jim suffered from TB in the stomach. Whilst the 99 percent had very little pain, Jim really suffered, and on the occasions when the severe pain was etched on his face and his brow was covered in beads of sweat, I almost felt sympathy pains with him. I don't know what treatment he was on, but I surmised it must be morphine administered to kill the pain. Meanwhile, my treatment was Albumin (called gold dust) and not albumen (egg white). This was preparatory to the treatment which was to follow and which would be with me for years to come. The injections were administered by Staff Nurse Cameron, who also gave Jim his treatment. I developed a temperature after my first injection, which seemed to surprise the medical staff as such an effect had never happened before, apparently. My fever persisted for about a week, after which things returned to normal and further injections followed without any more adverse reactions.

However, I had lost weight (which is always a dangerous thing with TB) and I was then prescribed a tablespoon of cod liver oil after each meal to help me regain weight. Cod liver oil taken neat is a horrible thing to take and initially makes one want to vomit, but in those circumstances some patients took it (and liked it) and some would even drink it straight from the bottle! But not me – I was finding it difficult enough to take the rice soup that we were served occasionally, with the multi-coloured (oil) skin floating on top. ARGHH! I did, however, gain weight and Jim and I returned to our normal routine.

One day, as we looked from our window to the peaceful, calm surroundings outside, Jim turned to me and said, "Do you realise there is a war going on – somewhere – with people being maimed and even killed and we're not even a small part of it. Here we are cosseted from it all, with three meals a day, care and attention and a warm bed at night. Do you not have any feelings of guilt and shame like me? We are just parasites, are we not?" I had never given any thought along those lines, but suddenly realised that Jim was simply echoing my own feelings in the matter. We had a comparatively easy life, compared to those in the 'outer world', but I said to Jim that I doubted very much whether any of them would willingly exchange their lifestyle for the unknown future that may await us, given the seriousness of our health problems. We had to some extent our own little Shangri-la where time really did seem to stand still. Seconds dragged into minutes, minutes into hours, hours into days, days into weeks, with the same monotonous routine, dulling our senses, with no peaks or troughs in our humdrum existence. We did exist – but were we living?

It took many years for me to overcome my feelings of guilt and shame, and I lived in dread of being asked the pointed question: "What did you do during the war?" What sort of reaction would my truthful reply of "Nothing" evoke?

Our existence was not helped by the isolation that we were subjected to, as on one occasion Jim said, "What sort of place is this, really?" Apart from the few members of staff (and our paper boy, old Haggerty) we never saw any other patients and although we sometimes glimpsed shadowy figures in the corridor and the occasional sound of movements, we were 'prisoner non-gratis'.

There were so many unanswered questions regarding even our most immediate surrounding:

What was the size and shape of the building?
How many rooms or wards were there?
How many patients were there in total?
How were they coping?
Was there a communal room, and if so were there seats for sitting in the sun, or shade?
Was there an assembly hall, and if so what size?
Was there a communal dining hall, and if so where? (I knew there was, as Jackie had gone for breakfast there).

I had a slight advantage over Jim, as I had spent a few days in the Monkey Run ward and met a few other patients, but Jim had been allocated his present bed on admission and had consequently seen nothing of the building whatsoever. I had been isolated on previous occasions – at the office, on lonely walks – whilst awaiting admission, and even comparative isolation in my previous ward, where conversation and fellowship were almost non-existent. For Jim, the isolation must have been even more acute and he must have felt more like being in a monastery than a hospital.

One night after 'lights-out', I got to thinking about my school pals who were serving in the forces – such as Harry, Billy, Joe, Jimmy, Adam and others – and even wondered how they were each feeling in their new experiences. Some of my other school pals were still at home, but working long hours in the steelworks, engineering works and factories, and having only Saturday afternoons off, did not have time to visit me, which was quite understandable.

Mail which we did receive was pretty much one-sided, as the incoming letters gave some details of life in the 'outer world', but our outgoing mail had very little to say, as nothing interesting ever seemed to happen or was worthy of writing about. Another day was over, let's just turn over and go to sleep.

Squeak! Squeak! Why don't they put some oil on the axle of the 'pan-loaf barrow' – the name given to the trolley with the domed canopy which was used to carry corpses to the mortuary situated in the grounds outside the main building.

Squeak! Squeak! Another patient, whom we had never met, made his final journey, now relieved of all his suffering.

Squeak! Squeak! A constant reminder of what may await us – a future however short or long, we knew not what – but Jim and I never thought that way – we were (probably mistaken) optimists, whose first aim was to survive and present an optimistic and cheerful record programme on San radio – not much ambition there! But from small acorns mighty oak trees grow!

Every morning, Sister would make her daily 'round' and on entering our room would welcome us with a cheerful "Good morning – how are we today?" Mustering up as much enthusiasm as we could, we would answer in unison, "Fine." Sister would then say, with reciprocal feigned enthusiasm, "You're coming along fine." This charade went on DAY after DAY after DAY after DAY after DAY – it was so monotonous, but it passed the time of day!

I had come to the conclusion that 'visiting hours' was simply a ploy to discourage friends from visiting. Have you ever sat through a one-sided dialogue for two hours? After ten minutes or so, after your visitor has given you all the news from the outside world, you have no real response. Do you tell them the highlight of your week: "The potatoes at dinner on Tuesday were cold!" Not much substance for discussion there, eh? The remaining one hour and 50 minutes was spent in embarrassing fidgeting!

There were no radiators or any heating in the building –

not even in the Duty Room – and the only place for warmth was the kitchen, or when you went for your 'regulated' bath time. During the winter months, when the weather could be quite severe, the staff were allowed the concession of being allowed to wear woollen cardigans (usually navy blue in colour) to keep out the cold. We patients just pulled the covers around ourselves as close as possible.

One morning, as Jim was sitting up in bed trying to read his *Glasgow Herald* with woollen-gloved hands trying to keep the pages from blowing away as the wind swept through the open windows and through the door jammed open by a wedge, he turned to me and said, "A nice cooling breeze this morning, Jack." I replied, "Y-Y-Yes, i-i-it is," stuttering with the cold.

And the same conditions prevailed at visiting times, so there was very little incentive for visitors to come and enjoy the 'healthy' conditions we were enjoying every day. When they were daft enough to endure the 'welcoming atmosphere', they had to be clad in heavy clothes, with scarf, woollen gloves – and I remember on one occasion, Mother wearing her fur coat (of which she was very proud) and woollen 'tammie' with a 'toorie' on top. She brought very little in the way of fruit, biscuits and sweets, all of which were on ration (and the San had my ration book!) but she did bring a Thermos flask containing tea, which she drank to keep herself warm. Chairs were at a premium and as there was no tearoom (or any other suitable accommodation for sitting), visitors sat on the edge of the bed. The strict rule of two visitors to a bed was never really enforced, as visitors never exceeded two anyway.

On one occasion, the local bus bringing visitors could only reach the gatehouse on the bottom avenue and could not climb the hill to the main gate due to the heavy snow fall, and all visitors had to trudge the remaining distance on foot and return the same way.

However, when patients began to progress to being allowed on their feet and the weather improved, they, and their visitors, could sit on the seats scattered around the grounds and visiting became a more pleasant experience.

<u>DAILY TIMETABLE FOR AN A/R (Absolute Rest) T.B. PATIENT</u>

7.15 -   Maid enters, lowers window sashes and switches on lights.

7.25 -   Nurse with basin of warm water for washing, on tray.

7.45 -   Breakfast.

8.30 -   Maid removes breakfast tray, and Nurse adjusts bedding.

8.45 -   Bed pan/bottle if required.

9.00 -   Maid switches off lights, raises window sashes and removes sputum mug and cleans, and replenishes fresh water jug.

9.10 -   Paper-boy arrives.

9.15 -   Sister's visit, with any mail. Tuesdays and Wednesdays we receive Sunday papers. Sister remarks 'you're doing fine'.

9.30 -   Staff nurse for any injections or medication - pulse, temperature and respiration reading.

10.00 -   **Rest hour** - complete silence, and no activity.

11.00 -   On Wednesdays, visit from Doctor, who hammers chest and back with cold stethoscope and states 'you're doing fine'.

11.15-12noon - **Free time** - eg. radio and reading.

12.00 -   Lunch - you know what day it is by the menu - Tuesday was always rice soup day!

12.30-14.00 -   **Free time** - reading, jigsaws, crosswords...

14.00-15.00 -   **Rest hour** - as before, we really need this as we are all *so* tired with all the activity of the day, so far!

22

15.00-16.15 -	**Free time** eg. writing and sketching.
16.30 -	Nurse for temperature, pulse and respiration. Maids prepare Black-out operation.
17.00 -	Dinner - you always knew it was Friday - fish to appease those of the catholic faith.
17.30-18.00 -	**Free time** - discussions with room-mates on the days 'activities' or any other subject.
18.00-19.00 -	'San' radio programme - verdict... 'boring!'
19.15-19.30 -	Nurse for temperature, pulse and respiration. Maid with supper - tea/warm milk and rich tea biscuit.
20.00 -	Lights out.
20.30 -	Night nurse enters, dressed in navy-blue cape with bright red trimmings, armed with a small hand torch (black-out) regulations must be observed.

The never-ending daily monotonous routine continued unabated until one Tuesday, on her daily round, Sister advised that as my present course of treatment was now over, I would receive the main treatment, starting the following day, and I would be moved to another room on the ground floor. I greeted this news with mixed feelings, for I knew I would be likely to make progress in combating my illness but I would also be leaving Jim and the pleasant times (considering the situations we were in) we had spent together.

I was prepared for surgery later that day and on Wednesday morning said my farewell to Jim, who wished me all the best for my future health and hoped we would meet again. I replied that as soon as I was fit enough and on my feet I would come and see him. Regrettably this never happened as he passed away some weeks later and I never saw him again. However, I have never forgotten him – he was a proper gentleman and a scholar and I am still indebted to him for all the encouragement he gave me, for the kindness he showed and even for the fun we shared together. I also strongly admired the spirit he demonstrated so forcibly during his trying times of severe pain, which he bore with such fortitude.

Sister had told me my treatment would be AP – short for artificial pneumo-thorax – and this would consist of having a needle inserted through the skin, between the ribs, and into the pleural cavity of the chest. Air would then be pumped in to partially collapse the affected lung so the disease could be made quiescent and the patient could then enjoy a good measure of future health. What she 'forgot' to tell me was that this type of treatment could go on for years – and it did! I was dressed in a loose theatre gown after having my armpit and chest shaved, covered by a blanket and seated in a wheelchair. As I was wheeled from the room I thought, 'At last I'll see something of this hospital.'

We went along the straight corridor and as I passed the various doors, I noticed they were wedged open like the one I had just left, and the rooms were occupied by bed-ridden patients. We carried on past the solarium (open to all the elements) – fresh air by the ton! All of this was on the right-hand side facing south, whilst on the other side were linen cupboards and storage rooms. After passing a small kitchen, we passed through the door leading to Pavilion 2. Along another short corridor with a staircase to the left (which I later discovered led to the main dining hall) and then a right turn into the theatre which was brightly lit, with a fully equipped operating table with overhead lights.

Present were Dr Baxter, the senior doctor for the hospital, the house doctor, Dr Teichman, theatre sister and Sister Simpson. Dr Baxter explained the procedure to be used and gave me a local anaesthetic in my right side. I was then placed on the operating table, turned on my left side and told to raise my right arm, placing my hand on my head to allow the skin to be taut, to clearly define the exact position of the ribs. I thought that with my slender build he wouldn't have any difficulty locating my ribs! The needle was then (painfully) inserted by Dr Baxter, who stood behind me, with Sister Simpson in front and Dr Teichman and the theatre sister close by. I then felt the sensation of air coming in and my lung beginning to collapse, but the greatest feeling was that I seemed to be having the very life squeezed out of me. "Just breathe normally," said Dr Baxter. I thought, 'How the heck can I breathe normally when you're squeezing it out of me,' (or so it seemed). There was a short pause and again more air was pumped in which caused me to perspire very heavily and Sister wiped my forehead with a swab and wiped a damp swab over my dry lips, at the same time squeezing my left hand saying, "You're doing fine." I didn't think so but didn't argue! "That's it," said Dr Baxter and although the whole procedure only took about 30 minutes, it felt like a lifetime.

I was then moved from the operating table and on to a trolley, covered by a blanket and returned to Pavilion 3, gasping for breath all the way. I passed Jim's room and entered 'the shelter', which was a circular wooden building at the end of the main building. It had no door but was accessed straight from the corridor. I was placed in the right-hand bed and noticed that there were five beds and five windows with the lower sashes open for fresh air and framed by dark heavy curtains. The pain was excruciating and my only thought was, 'Just leave me alone, and let me die peacefully.' But it was not to be (fortunately).

A short time later another patient was wheeled in who also came from the theatre. His name was Bob Stevenson. He was in the same state as me and kept saying, between gasps for air, "This is murder." Welcome to the club!

Bob had been a policeman in Glasgow police, and regularly on duty at the seven-road junction at Bridgeton Cross, constantly reminding us that he was the only constable capable of keeping the traffic flowing at this oft-times bottleneck. Over the next few weeks, he kept reminding us of it so often that one day I said, "When I get out of here I'm going to join the Glasgow police and get the points duty at Bridgeton Cross as I know absolutely everything there is to know about it."

The other three patients in 'the shelter' were on different stages of AP and assured us that in a week's time our breathing pattern would return to normal. A week's time? – If I survived that long! I did not take any lunch or tea or even a glass of water or even a glass of milk at supper. I could not get to sleep at night and asked the night nurse for a sleeping draught. She, in turn, went to see Night Sister Dewar, who, although I had been in the hospital for several weeks, I had never seen. She was in her late forties, plump and had the air of a future matron. This was the first time we had met and would be the last time until I saw her again on the night prior to my leaving hospital many months later under entirely different circumstances! Her first question was to ask me what all the fuss was about, and I replied that I had only asked for a sleeping draught, to which she replied, "Don't be such a big moaner!" Others had come through this *little* pain without complaint. "You don't need a sleeping draught." So much for Matron's initial talk about receiving the best of care and attention!

I must have slept fitfully, because about 6.30am I was awakened by the night nurse with a basin of lukewarm water for washing and shaving. I said I did not know if I could shave properly because of the discomfort on my right side – to which she replied that by not shaving I was lowering the high standards of hygiene expected of the establishment. I then proceeded to have the worst shave I have ever had! I took no meals that day, but before 'lights out' had a glass of warm milk.

The following morning I took a little porridge at about 9am and then two nurses arrived with wheelchairs – one for me and one for Bob. When I asked where we were going, they replied (almost gleefully I thought), "You're going for a refill," and we were wheeled along to the theatre for treatment, similar to the previous occasion. Surprisingly, this was not so painful – in fact the extra air being pumped in did not increase the pain or make me short of breath. Over the weekend there was, naturally, no treatment, but it resumed again on the Monday and thereafter at regular intervals. By the Wednesday the other patients' predictions came true, because although still very conscious of having air in my cavity, breathing was returning to normal again.

Looking out from one of the windows one day I observed four chalets adjacent to the block, and discovered each was occupied by two all-day patients. They strictly observed the morning and afternoon rest periods. They obviously went for their three meals a day in the main dining hall, but I had no contact with them.

With the fresh air coming in through the five open windows, I caught a cold and was given much attention as they did not want this to develop into 'flu. This was something they feared as such an epidemic would have caused chaos and would have literally closed the whole place down. Fortunately, during my whole stay, no cases of 'flu were ever reported – I think the fresh air treatment blew them all away!

During the next two to three weeks, I progressed steadily until one morning Sister on her round announced that from the following day I would be on B1. This for me was like being told I had won the football pools – it meant farewell to bed pans. The system of monitoring one's progress was by the following scale:

B1:	Up at 7.30am to bathroom for ablutions and return to bed for breakfast – you regulated your bowel movements to meet the scale of progress!
B2:	As above, plus to bathroom between 11.45am and 12 noon.
B3:	As above, plus to bathroom between 4.45pm and 5pm.
B4:	As above, plus to bathroom between 7.15pm and 7.30pm.
Lights out:	8pm prompt.
One Hour:	Between 8am and 9am.
Two Hours:	Between 8am and 10am and to dining hall for breakfast.
Three Hours:	As above, plus 11 am to 12 noon.
Four Hours:	As above, plus noon until 1pm and lunch at dining hall.
Five Hours:	As above, plus 3pm to 4 pm.
Six Hours:	As above, plus to dining hall for tea.
All day (A/D):	Being all day from 7.30am till 8pm less the two rest periods, 10am till 11am and 2pm till 3pm when everything literally closed down – except on Saturdays when visiting was from 2pm till 4 pm.

I made good progress and within a few weeks had gone from B1 to One Hour and this gave me the opportunity to visit the recreation room on the ground floor. The first room I had been in (called the Monkey Run) was a large room and formed part of the tower structure of the building. The room below that was called the 'Model' due to its resemblance to establishments of that nature in Glasgow, and was of similar size. The recreation room was again of similar dimensions and again had a high ceiling, but with heavy curtains. Only the Monkey Run and the Model had black-painted window panes – all the other rooms and corridors had heavy curtains.

The most striking feature of the recreation room was a three-quarter-size billiards table. The other furnishings consisted of a roll-top writing bureau, a piano (much in need of tuning) and dart board (at regulation height), a unit of three or four shelves of library books (built up over many years and covering almost every subject), a table top for jigsaws, two small tables for chess and draughts (but no playing cards!), four straight-back chairs and a bay window looking out onto the San grounds.

I promptly asked Mother not to bring me any more books from Hamilton Library as I started to use the 'rec' library and also the jigsaws, some of which had stickers on showing the shortest time taken by a previous patient to complete the whole picture, competition being one of the principal means of sustaining interest in keeping alive a vestige of survival in an otherwise dull and tedious existence.

CHAPTER 5

The Three Musketeers

One day Sister informed me that I had progressed to Two Hours status and with effect from the following day, was being moved to the 'Blue Room' on the first floor. I ascended the stairs (this time at San pace) and arrived at an open door immediately adjacent to the Model. The room consisted of four beds and the first thing I noticed was that the walls were painted pastel green – why was a 'blue' room painted green? The other three occupants of the room were just preparing for rest hour and I promptly asked the question, to be told that the room was called 'Blue' because it was occupied by Sister Simpson's 'blue-eyed boys' – so why was I here?

The three occupants were:

Dick Moss, a man in his late 20s who came from Rutherglen and had been a maintenance engineer at Templeton's carpet factory in Bridgeton.

Bill Carrigan, aged mid-30s, from Maryhill, who had been manager in a '50-bob' tailors in the centre of Glasgow. He was always immaculately dressed (no clothing ration books with Bill).

Finally, there was Joe McGowan, aged 35-40, who was a chartered accountant from Motherwell.

We all settled down for the rest hour which, when ended,

produced a sound I had never heard since coming into the San – LAUGHTER! The banter between the three was quite infectious and I soon found myself actually enjoying it. They were called the 'Three Musketeers' and were practically a law unto themselves – but never breaking any San rules – just bending them a little! This was my first introduction to 'positive thinking' for their philosophy on life was: 'There *is* life after TB – live for today and tomorrow will look after itself – it may even be better!' The whisky bottle was always half full – never half empty – although none of them actually drank. There was always a positive side to every situation, no matter what the circumstances. Life in the San began to take on a new meaning for me – I made up my mind – I was going to join them!

The following morning they took me on my first visit to the dining hall in Pavilion 2 for breakfast. This we entered by a door separate from the female patients, and sat at tables sectioned off from the opposite sex, for fraternisation was strictly taboo. This was one rule strictly adhered to as everyone had other things on their minds – normally trying to beat this debilitating disease and get home as soon as possible – incentive enough on its own.

I very rarely saw the Three Musketeers because Dick and Bill were on Six Hours and Joe was A/D (all day) and all had been allocated certain duties – Dick to assist the San gardener – Bill to attend to the needs of the bed-bound patients in the solarium (delivering and collecting mail, supplying books and jigsaws etc) – whist Joe was employed in the San office doing all the administration work and it was only after lights out we had time for discussion and (heated) debate! Dick was a Christian Scientist and read the Bible religiously every day. Bill was an atheist and Joe was an agnostic – what a motley crew to be saddled with! I was just a young Presbyterian with practically no knowledge of life as such. Having seemingly nothing else to discuss, any debate would centre around religion – or the lack of it – and sometimes became quite heated with each of these strong-willed individuals insisting they were right – except me – (I just listened). However, all was sweetness and light in the morning as their motto was 'One for all and all for one – brothers together'.

I noticed that on her daily rounds, Sister spent more time in the Blue Room than anywhere else and this led to a rumour that Joe and she were in a liaison, as he spent most of his day in her office on his administration duties – but Dick and Bill ridiculed such a suggestion, having all been some very close friends for some considerable time, and I never had any reason to doubt them.

I told them of my notion to take over the duties of presenter on the San radio programme and was going to ask Sister if she could possibly change my Two Hours to 9-10am and 6-7pm, which suggestion brought gales of laughter from the three. However, I did approach Sister, who informed me that I would need to be Six Hours before consideration, but when I reached Four Hours she might re-consider – I felt I might yet become a blue-eyed boy!

As well as their allotted duties, the three always found time to walk (although never in the areas of the grounds reserved for use by female patients) and sometimes resorted to going 'out of bounds' to the river Gryffe, which flowed quite close by where they tried fishing. Unfortunately the only thing they ever caught was a cold! They did persevere, however, having been told by someone that there were trout in the river. I don't think they ever intended to catch anything – it was purely an exercise to pass time and enjoy an escapade away from the restrictions of the San regime.

I continued to make good progress health-wise and

heartened by my new companionship made my next landmark of Three Hours and subsequently Four Hours – so this was it, down to the Duty Room immediately to see Sister and remind her of her 'promise' to consider my request. She told me the decision was not hers alone, but she would let me know as soon as possible. A week dragged by and then she gave me good news – that as the presenter was due to be going home shortly, I would be considered. I got the confirmation and passed the news to the three immediately.

"Right," said Joe, "let's have a good look at this place," because none of us had seen the radio room before. It was at the end of the corridor on the second floor and so we all climbed the flight of stairs (at San pace), arriving at the door that we noticed had a red light above it. This was lit by a switch inside and indicated when broadcasting was taking place to keep intruders out. (This phrase is of great importance and will also be of even greater importance later on!)

CHAPTER 6

A Dream Come True

As we opened the door, we saw what was in essence Aladdin's cave – for it contained hundreds of records, all beautifully arranged and numbered. It had obviously been built up over many years and contained full operas, symphonies and every other type of music from Scottish dance to modern jazz, and solo singers from operas to music hall artistes. I even found a record by the great Italian tenor Enrico Caruso which, when we played it, was almost perfect in sound reproduction and had it come up for auction would have raised hundreds of pounds.

Along one wall was a bench on which were two turntables and two microphones of the BBC type; square frames with round microphones inset and stems for hand-held use. There were dozens of boxes of needles and two leather-bound books, one of which showed all the records in numerical order and had been written up over many years as could be seen by the different handwriting. The other book had been divided into sections and cross-referenced to the numbers to show the different categories, eg: classical, soloists, dance, brass bands etc, covering almost every aspect of music and covering many years of recordings.

The reason the range was so extensive was because each month every patient paid one penny into the 'record fund' to buy new records which were chosen by an elected 'record committee'. All three pavilions were represented on this committee and their selection was bought, usually at Biggars, the large record shop in Glasgow, who themselves sometimes donated one or two records popular at the time. The bigger records of classical music must have been donated over the years by generous ex-patients and their relatives or friends.

We took the two record books down to the Blue Room to check exactly what was available as we decided the new programme must be bright and cheery to send out a clear message that there was life with TB and even after hospitalisation.

The Three Musketeers told me I had to open the programme with a cheery "Good morning and a warm welcome to the new-style record request programme!" I was also to use some of Carrigan's humorous one-liners to give it some impact. We also decided to use signature tunes from the vast number of records available. We chose *Blue Room* by the Ambrose Orchestra, which opened the morning session, and we closed with *Here's to the Next Time* by Henry Hall and his orchestra. The evening session was opened by Jack Payne and his orchestra and closed with *Goodnight Sweetheart* by an American band with the closing remark. "I'll be with you tomorrow – don't be late!"

Before this there had never been any voice-overs and there had been long gaps between the records, for the presenter seemed to pick the requested records from the shelves as he went along. We decided to give continuity by having the records already laid out in the sequence requested and this would be arranged by Moss replacing each record in its correct position after use. At the end of the first week we awaited the verdict on the new format and the feedback was that it had been a complete success. Encouraged by this, I began to ask our 'listeners' to write any anecdotes, short limericks or jokes to keep growing interest from all and such was the response that we were completely overwhelmed by San mail.

The previously agreed arrangement was that each room, in sequence, would choose the programme (and this we continued) and to do this, the books had to go to allow their particular choice to be made (in the female's cases to Pavilions 1 and 2) and be returned to the radio room for compilation. Sister made contact (at our request) with Margaret McCallum, who had been a primary school teacher, asking her to give any little (confidential) gossip which may interest the girls – and this she did with notes included in the books when returned, so that a little 'tittle-tattle' was included with the record requests. The girls got quite chuffed at getting a mention on air but Margaret's name was kept strictly confidential and never divulged, which added further intrigue to the question "Who supplied the information?" The criteria for the whole programme was our initial slogan that it must be cheerful, bright and optimistic – so much so that Sister on her morning round one day remarked that there seemed to be a marked change in the whole atmosphere about the place, which prompted McGowan to remark, "Goodbye gloom and doom – hello humour and fun!" Every morning in our Blue Room we began our day with chanting our slogan: "Every day in every way, I am getting better." It was crazy but it seemed to work – positive thinking was shining through!

The programme had now become more of a record and chat show than anything else and seemed to get the approval of all patients. I had been proposing further changes such as a 'brains trust' quiz, short stories and a programme called *Know thy Neighbour* (all in the evenings) to create more interest, but the Musketeers rejected these ideas as being too ambitious and infeasible to arrange as some patients were not able to participate due to being in the early stages of recuperation and were not 'available' in the evenings. Then Carrigan came in all excited: "I've just met a chap in the solarium who I think could be a great addition to our team. His name is Jim Boyd and although he is only One Hour, he could help us with the scripts etc, as he was a prominent member of an amateur dramatic society in Glasgow.

We all trooped down to see this 'genius' who told us he had been employed as a senior official with Glasgow Corporation and produced shows in amateur theatre. He was mid-30s, had been through college and looked the ideal type to integrate with the Musketeers' thinking – though not quite so zany! I mentioned that I had been thinking of changing the programme format, giving my suggestions, to which he replied that he had also been thinking of ideas along similar lines. He said we should consider producing a radio magazine programme incorporating as many ideas as possible. All sorts of ideas were suggested and at the end of our meeting we all agreed that we should ask patients to come up with a suitable title for the programme, which would be broadcast one evening per week. I announced our proposals during the following morning's programme and from the huge response we received, the title *San Fairy An* was chosen and adopted – don't ask me what it means, because I don't know! As an experiment, we decided to have someone read a book and after agreement an abridged version of *The Master of Ballantrae* was chosen with one or two chapters being read each evening.

Mcgowan suggested that 'JimBo' be given the job but as

he was only on One Hour this presented a problem. McGowan then said we should approach Sister to seek her special permission for JimBo to change his One Hour from 8-9am to 6-7pm for one week or so only, We hoped he could persuade Sister, aided and abetted by Carrigan with his charming ways. It was with some relief that they reported back having been successful.

This innovation led to the *San Fairy An* programme, which consisted of records and also topics (though not broadcast on the same evening). The programme was broadcast once a week with the script being written by JimBo. McGowan agreed to present the first programme and included a short story. I had contacted Jackie who was now on A/D and was due to be discharged the following week and asked him if he would do the first story, and after some tuition from JimBo, he agreed. He was really pleased – fame at last! The next programme was called *Know Thy Neighbour*, and I had contacted a chap called Davans who had been with the International Brigade during the Spanish Civil War and was a suitable candidate. After tuition by JimBo, he gave his reminiscences of that conflict – again a successful first. A chap called Armstrong, who had been a detective in Glasgow police, followed on the next programme and others followed in successive weeks.

I was still doing my record request programme but not taking part in *San Fairy An,* having left the others to get on with it. Every week it was introducing new voices (and ideas) and was becoming almost a full time job, with patients participating who, previously, would never have considered such a thing. The whole place had taken on an air of optimism and hope for the future and a general togetherness never seen before. I was beginning to feel that I didn't want to leave the place – well not quite!

I was meeting regularly with JimBo for elocution lessons and picked up many hints, which stood me in good stead in future years. McGowan was also giving me lessons on cost accounting, giving me certain exercises to do and generally widening my limited knowledge of office management and financial matters appertaining to certain aspects of business procedures – and he was a hard task-master!

It was the custom, one Sunday each month, for a church service to be held in the main hall, separate from the main building and which all patients on Two Hours and more were expected to attend. (For 'expected' read 'must' for *we have ways and means to make you do so*). This was more a religious meeting rather than a service and was conducted by a lay-preacher who came over from Quarriers' homes. The service consisted of two well-known hymns or psalms, two readings from the bible, a solo by a female patient, a solo by a male patient, a talk by the lay-preacher, two prayers, benediction and a collection. Most patients resented being forced to attend and some, including the Three Musketeers, objected strongly (Moss on the grounds that he had his own 'style' of religion – namely Christian Science) – but everyone attended!

The female patients entered by the main door and occupied the seats on the right-hand side whilst the men entered by the side door nearest our pavilion and sat on the left – with a wide passageway between both groups. Matron sat in the front row, accompanied by some members of the nursing staff with any maids or others behind. At the end of the meeting, the women returned by 'their' door, followed a few minutes later by the men through 'their' door.

After one meeting, I approached the lay-preacher and asked if I could possibly visit the Quarriers' church, which was well-known in the area for its architectural features (my reason being more out of curiosity rather than any religious fervour), and he agreed to meet me for an evening service sometime in the future when I was on A/D. I approached Sister to obtain her permission to go. She agreed, cautioning me to be discreet in the matter.

The following Sunday, I left after tea and made my way by the bottom avenue and through the gate leading to the village, which was only a few minutes' walk away where I met my preacher friend. As we entered the village, I immediately noticed how neat and tidy the grounds were kept, with beds of roses and other flowers with not a weed to be seen. As we approached the church, which was of grey stone, I saw groups of children aged from about five to 16 walking in pairs, the younger taking hands and escorted by the house-parents. All were well disciplined, well dressed and behaving in an immaculate manner. They were obviously subjected to the same discipline as in the San.

Many years later I saw the same discipline during visits to Russia. I saw the same discipline in children, but taken to extreme measure, as I never saw a misbehaved child during my time in that country.

The minister who conducted the service was quite elderly and obviously had been brought out of retirement to fill the vacancy created by a shortage of ministers due to the war. The interior of the church was in keeping with the whole village, being neat and tidy with all furnishings beautifully polished. After the service, I thanked my friend for the courtesy extended to me and bade him farewell. I then returned to the San by a circular route to avoid detection and well before lights out. I must have been the only patient from the San to visit Quarriers' homes village, although this was never made known.

CHAPTER 7

Arrivals and Departures

One day, we were visited in the Blue Room by wee Frank Konchater, a Jew, who had just been promoted to Two Hours and who was expected to attend church services – to which he unsuccessfully protested. He then came to us to seek advice. McGowan and Carrigan immediately informed him that they would be delighted to take up his case with Sister, and using their combined persuasion and charm techniques, were hopeful of a successful result. However, when they approached Sister, she informed them that she could not give such a decision as she felt it would require to be taken up by a higher authority, since it may set a precedent to be exploited in the future. McGowan said that Sister appreciated the position, but as a compromise Konchater could undertake any voluntary work during the hour's service (not telling Frankie!) and nothing further was said until the Friday before the next service when the compromise was agreed.

McGowan then went to Frankie to give him the news and tell him he would be required to work in the main kitchen, up to his elbows in soap suds washing dishes etc and generally helping the maids. To McGowan's relief, Frankie instantly agreed, not realising that for the rest of his stay in the San every fourth Sunday would be spent on 'sink duties'.

McGowan was told a week or so later that he was being discharged and we said our farewells with the usual good wishes for continued good health and hoped that we would meet again and renew 'auld acquaintance'. In fact, a few years later, I did meet him again at a business meeting in Motherwell and was delighted to see that he was, indeed, in robust good health.

This meant that there now was a 'vacancy' for a third Musketeer, and the other two teased me about holding a mock election to see who could fill the post. However, in the end common sense prevailed and I was admitted as an 'honorary member' and replied by giving a 'thank you' speech. I moved into McGowan's bed, and we then welcomed a new roommate in the person of John McCafferty. He was in his early 20s, and had been a radio operator in the RAF. He had blonde hair, almost snowy white, which seemed to make him look older than his years. He was quite a quiet individual, and although a nice fellow companion, was not the boisterous type like us. John was an RC, and for some reason or another the 'after night' discussions were never renewed. We only saw John at the rest periods, because now all on A/D, we were otherwise 'employed' in various duties. I had taken over some of the administration duties, previously done by McGowan, and worked with Sister some of the time, although I also assisted Moss and the gardener, potting plants and tidying up around the area of the grounds, whilst Carrigan was still distributing and collecting mail, collecting books and jigsaws etc, to those bed-ridden patients in the solarium and ground floor, playing chess and draughts with them and generally trying to keep their spirits up. We were all active between the hours of 7.30am and 8pm (less rest hours) and were enjoying our status in the San.

Being all on A/D, we joined together to go on some afternoons for our five-mile walk, which was really out of bounds, in parts, and on one occasion I witnessed the other side of the Quarrier's coin. We were re-entering the grounds, passing the gatehouse cottage, when we heard a child crying rather loudly and noticed the male house-parent striking a boy in the back garden. Carrigan immediately broke San pace and opening the gate to the cottage uttered, "I'm going to get that b******!" going around the rear of the cottage to confront him. Moss and I followed and took the boy, who was about eight or nine, aside and comforted him by drying his tears and calming him down, as he was shaking badly. Carrigan was, meantime, standing eye-to-eye with the house-parent and adopting a threatening attitude. Moss then interrupted to calm things down by separating them, whilst the man shouted that we had no right to interfere, since we were trespassing outwith our allotted area of ground. I led Carrigan over to the boy as Moss, in a very quiet but firm voice, told the man that if we so wished, we could report him for his manner of treatment of the boy, and that he was prepared to take this to the highest authority, regardless of what would happen to us. In his earlier years, Moss had been an amateur boxer (although not very good, he admitted), but his calm demeanour was such that harmony was quickly restored. Moss made the point, very firmly, that we passed this way regularly and would be watching carefully for any further trouble that could lead to closer investigation. The situation was quickly resolved, with handshakes all round – but we did keep a watchful eye on the peace in our future walks, although nothing further occurred.

We then had a dilemma about whether we should report the incident, as Carrigan was still incensed by what had happened, but after discussion, we decided it might be better to declare the matter closed. We never told anyone, but kept it entirely to ourselves.

About this time, a new patient was admitted called Phil Cox, who had been skipper of a merchant ship, which had been torpedoed in the Atlantic. He and his crew had spent several days in an open boat, before being rescued and landed at Greenock, from where he finished up in the San. He did not seem to suffer from TB and never seemed to spend much time in his bed. It seemed to us that he was really only with us to recover from his terrible ordeal in the open sea. He was about 6ft tall and had been first violin and then conductor of the Bexhill-on-Sea light orchestra. He was seen on many occasions wearing his white polo-neck jumpers, as all his other belongings had been lost at sea, although the San did supply other clothing. We never really met him, but from whatever source, he had obtained a violin, which he practiced in the recreation room, much to the annoyance of the patients who were using the room. However, this only lasted a short time and he later practiced outdoors. On his travels in the San he had managed to recruit another three 'musicians' in the persons of Archie Roy on piano, Alex Rankin on percussion, and a chap called Myles on mandolin. Archie Roy was later a professor at Glasgow University, and author of several novels (I still have the full set in my possession). Myles was from Kilmarnock, and had TB in the arm, and had been in Shotts Sanatorium, before being transferred to us. His arrival had created a story that was never confirmed as fact or fiction by either of the parties involved. On arrival at the Duty Room, Sister asked him his name. He replied, "I'm Myles from Shotts," to which Sister said, "I know you're miles from Shotts, but what's your name?" We reckoned Myles had made it up, and although Sister never made any comment, she certainly knew of the story, and we knew her sense of fun was such that it may have been true. (See reference to this episode, later.)

Cox had now got his band for rehearsals, although I don't know how he managed musical arrangements for such a motley crew – they were certainly no threat to Max Jaffa and his Palm Court Orchestra! After their first session I asked Carrigan how they got on. His answer was, "Loud, if not good," but they did improve and featured in a project later.

More patients were volunteering their services and taking over as presenter after coaching by JimBo, which meant I was spending less time 'on air'. One such volunteer was Willie Highet, who asked to present a programme called *Bing and Swing* which consisted of the many records of Bing Crosby and American bands such as Benny Goodwin, Count Basie and Duke Ellington etc. Willie was well versed in these, having got all his information from a music magazine that he received every week. He came from Kilmarnock and had a typical Ayrshire accent and droll sense of humour. This he communicated well in his presentation, which seemed to please everyone and it turned out to be the best programme on air. Many years later, on a visit to America, he made a point of tracing and meeting some of the musicians who'd participated in these record sessions.

CHAPTER 8

Outside Broadcasts

Although I was no longer 'broadcasting', I was still thinking of new ideas, which I discussed with Moss and Carrigan, who gave me their support. I noticed that all broadcasts were being conducted indoors so I thought, 'Why not experiment with outside broadcasts?' I approached Sister with my idea and she said she didn't see any objection to this, although a cable would need to be led down the outside of the building from the radio room to ground level. There was only one problem – we did not have a cable long enough for the job! I went to see our mutual friend, Konchater, and asked if among his many connections in Glasgow South-side, he could get a length of suitable cable for our use. He asked what length I needed, and as I didn't know, I contacted Don Wilson (who had been a surveyor) and together with Frankie we all agreed on a suitable length which we considered ample – with a few extra feet, just in case. Frankie said, "Leave it with me," and about a fortnight later, appeared with a huge roll of cable. I asked him how much it was going to cost, to which he replied, "Actually, it fell off the back of a lorry." We couldn't have got it much cheaper than that!

The next thing was to get it connected up to one of our microphones, to see if it really worked. McCafferty was given the task and spent several of his two-hour stints testing, altering and re-testing until he declared he *thought* it would work. During his testing of the whole system he informed us that he had discovered that on the main control panel, certain sections of the system could be cut off from the radio and that would allow us to broadcast without Pavilions 1 and 2 being tuned in (INTERESTING! – see later.) We gave the system a test run and it proved successful.

Snooker had become quite popular even among those who had not had a misspent youth and I decided this would be a worthwhile event to broadcast. A match was organised between Bradley (who had been the West of Scotland amateur snooker champion a few years before he was admitted to the San) and Tommy Kinnaird, who was the next best player from among all the other eligible players. The game would be played between 3pm and 5pm. and Moss had arranged with both players that they play as slowly as possible to allow the commentator (namely yours truly) sufficient time to get his 'lines' right. He also arranged that to give the programme some atmosphere, the spectators would applaud each shot and I would from time to time ask some of the 'crowd' for their views on what shots could or should be played. I thought all you needed to do was pot the balls, but Highet put me right on that score by telling me that it was a game of tactics as well as skill. I therefore arranged that he would stand beside me and after I had described each shot played, I invited him to give his opinion on the strategy in the progress of the game.

We were pleasantly surprised that everything went so well. The general consensus was that it was a huge success and that more games should be broadcast for the benefit of the bed-ridden patients. It was my first (and last) broadcast of a snooker match because I gave the job to Highet, who was much better at it than me, but it had been another success story in the fight against tedium and boredom!

My next idea was to broadcast putting and this really was an 'outside' broadcast. The putting green stretched from the path outside the building down to the bottom avenue and consisted of nine holes on the slope, but when I checked the view from the summer seat, which was as far as our cable would stretch, only some of the holes could be fully seen as bushes and shrubs obscured the view. I then contacted Don Wilson to see if he could re-design the course so that all nine holes could be seen from the vantage point. When asking a favour, we always finished by stating, "You're doing nothing else anyway," or "You've plenty of time on your hands to do it," and in all cases they were only too happy to co-operate, giving them an interest. So Don got out his measuring tape and sketchpad and after a couple of days produced a new course. This meant quite a re-arrangement of almost all the holes, but the gardener readily agreed and Moss was given the job of cutting the new holes with the tool made for that purpose and painting the cups with white paint.

For the first broadcast, he (Moss) also arranged for the 'gallery' of spectators to applaud each shot and I had to involve the onlookers by asking them for their comments on the match, which was between Don himself and Kinnaird, these two being the best players. I did the commentary, assisted by Highet and the venture was declared another success. It was my first 'golf' broadcast (and last!), as Don took on the mantle of commentator for all the matches in the putting competition.

My big idea of outside broadcasting was to have a lengthy one on croquet, which was played mostly by the A/D patients and could be played between 9am and 10am and 11am and 12 noon. Also between 1pm to 2pm and between 3pm to 5pm.

Some games stretched to two or even three days – like cricket test matches! Competition for a regular slot for playing was keen and in some instances almost led to 'fisticuffs' – you had to let your frustration out somehow! One of the sources of trouble was a chap called Kenny Hunter who was never off the lawn and was really the Stephen Hendry of the croquet lawn. Anyone who partnered him was always on a winning team. Croquet is also a game of tactical skills and an ability to use the mallet and balls with physical dexterity. Unfortunately, Hunter had a tendency to use somewhat dubious gamesmanship to enable him to be always a winner – but a loser with all the other players, who resented his attitude, so much so we had to write to some organisation (not Wimbledon) for a rule book which, in fact, caused more bother over interpretation than it solved in straightforward disputes.

The croquet lawn was regulation size, consisting of four hoops and two pins with four different coloured balls and mallets. It was on a level grass-covered surface, except for one corner, which fell away to a hollow. This was called 'Hell Corner' by us, for it was quite difficult to extricate the balls from this area without incurring a penalty. Hunter exploited this situation regularly by manoeuvring his opponents into this hazard, which almost certainly resulted in their defeat.

There was only one thing wrong with my idea for broadcasting croquet – as we prepared for our first programme, we discovered that the cable wasn't long enough! I therefore again approached wee Frankie for his assistance, and as usual, without any apparent bother, he again produced a further length of cable. This, yet again, had fallen off the back of a lorry – a different lorry, perhaps? McCafferty then connected up the parts and after testing the system declared it 'all clear' for broadcasting.

Moss did not need to arrange a gallery or any atmosphere, for all who were eligible to attend were there and any comments from them required no prompting as everyone was an 'expert' in the game. I asked Highet to be with me as scorer because the game consisted of striking (or 'taking' as was the terminology) the balls by the use of the mallet and this had to be noted so that each player would abide by the rules. This could, however, lead to many arguments about whose ball had 'taken' the others in the course of going through the hoops and striking the pins. Don drew up a chart for Highet to use in order to keep score of the takings in each part of the game as it progressed.

A small non-member committee had been formed in order to create interest in the game, to adjudicate in procedures and any disputes which may (and often did) arise. The committee decided that on this 'historic' occasion of first broadcast, the game would be played between 3pm and 5pm in the afternoon each afternoon until the final stroke was made. The teams chosen were Hunter and the poorest player versus Kinnaird and Carrigan, who were considered to be the next best pair in the pecking order as far as ability was concerned. The game began at 3pm and actually lasted three days – two hours each day (it was like a cricket test match!) – such was the competition. The outcome, however, was predictable – Kinnaird and Carrigan were just not good enough!

During the game, Highet would update on the score (or takings) and I would ask some of the spectators for their comments. On one occasion this led to a rather rash observation by Alex Rankin, who when asked to comment on the problem of getting out of Hell Corner, remarked casually, "It's not something to think *about* they need, but something to think *with* to get out of Hell corner – the stupid idiots!" The remark was picked up by someone in authority and I was severely reprimanded for allowing a word such as 'Hell' to be broadcast on the air (and never let it happen again!)

This was (again) my first and last broadcast on croquet, as I notified the committee that my office duties were such that I had no time to continue and so they held a meeting to decide who should do the job. Carrigan proposed Hunter, much to the chagrin of the others, but strangely his proposal carried the day. Hunter was then asked to take the position and promptly accepted. This ploy was part of Carrigan's nefarious scheme, for he knew that if Hunter was broadcasting, he was not playing and this would give the others a better chance of an evenly matched game. Hunter only realised this after about a week and resigned as commentator, to be succeeded by Tommy Kinnaird.

CHAPTER 9

The Pantomime

About a fortnight later, during one of our 'after eight' evening discussions, Moss made the comment that we now had enough talent available to present a stage concert, which we others in the Blue Room considered to be just a little too ambitious and that it would never be accepted by the authorities (whoever they were – we never found out!)

However, next morning, Moss and Carrigan went to see JimBo, who was now on Two Hours, to discuss the possibilities of such a venture. He immediately agreed it was possible and said that he would arrange all the details for such a production, provided they could overcome the main obstacle – permission to do so! Moss and Carrigan then went to see Sister, to give her all the reasons why this should happen; namely it would be a morale booster for the whole place, with as many as possible participating, both on and off stage, and would lift everyone's spirits. Sister, as usual, counselled caution but agreed to put their proposals to a higher level. A long two days ensued before she gave them the 'all clear', and immediately a small committee was formed (again I excluded myself on the grounds of being too busy), with JimBo being in charge.

The decision was taken that the show should take the form of a pantomime, with solo acts between the scenes and should only run for about one to one-and-a-half hours maximum. Wee Frankie volunteered the information that he was acquainted with Jack Anthony – who was a Scottish comedian and played all the theatres with his company – and he would ask him to supply us with any scripts and/or suitable clothing for an all-male cast. A response was received about ten days later and together with make-up and clothing supplied by the women in Pavilions 1 and 2, who had been contacted by Sister, things began to gather momentum. The script by Jack Anthony was for *Cinderella* and whilst some of it was suitable, JimBo decided it would need to be altered considerably to make it more topical for the San's use. Jack Anthony had also supplied Frankie with some music, and this was passed to Phil Cox for his arrangements.

The cast was chosen, with the principals being Don Wilson (at 6ft 2in) as Cinderella, and Frankie (at 5ft 2in) as Prince Charming – an ideally suited pair! Moss and I played the ugly sisters (inspirational casting – and quite appropriate – Moss with his broken nose from his boxing days, and me with my two front teeth missing!) and rehearsals began. We had no scenery, so a table and mock-up cooking range were used for the kitchen scene, and small tables and chairs with fancy covers for the ballroom scene, so there were really only two acts. The other acts consisted of two songs by a girl from Pavilion 2, two songs by Charlie McIntosh from his police choir repertoire, a short selection of tunes by Phil Cox on violin, two tunes on mandolin by Myles and a grand finale by Anne-Marie Kelly from Pavilion 1. Anne-Marie was an accordionist and had been semi-professional on the halls, sometimes with Jack Anthony, and she 'brought the house down' with a selection of sing-along songs to finish off the whole evening. A maid from Pavilion 2 had a printer friend from Paisley who produced an A4 single sheet programme showing the concert was being presented by 'The Pavilion Players' with guests – the guests being the two females from the other pavilions.

On the evening of the show, which began at 6pm, the women entered by their usual door and the men by theirs with Matron and other members of staff seated in the front row and the 'Phil Cox Quartet' in front and to the right of the stage. Dr Baxter introduced the show jocularly saying that it was being presented here before going on Scottish tour. Things generally went well, with one or two expected hitches, one of which was when Myles wandered on to the stage with a lost look on his face, to be asked by one of the cast, "Who are you?" – to which he replied, "I'm miles from Shotts." This prompted the adjoiner: "Well if you hurry, you'll be just in time to catch the bus at the San gates in about five minutes!" Sister thoroughly enjoyed the irony of this, but it was completely lost on all the others. On another occasion, when the leader of the 'orchestra' was mentioned, one of the cast struck a theatrical pose saying, "TB or not TB, that is the question, for him." Again the irony was lost on most of the audience. After Anne-Marie's rousing finale, we all took our (deserved?) bow.

The Matron then gave a vote of thanks to all concerned in the production for all their efforts and hoped the evening's entertainment would act as an encouragement for all patients in their recovery to future good health. The women then exited by their door and the men, later, by theirs.

On returning to our pavilion, the Three Musketeers, accompanied by Highet, Wilson and Konchater, returned to the Pavilion 3 kitchen to celebrate. This consisted of tins of pilchards, which had been brought in by Highet's mother over two or three visits, and with toast (and real butter) we tucked in to our real feast with mugs of hot tea. The verdict – DELICIOUS! To us it was like dining at the Ritz – well maybe not quite (as none of us had ever been to the Ritz).

About a week later, during the afternoon rest hour, I got to thinking about how things had changed so dramatically since well over two years previously when I entered the zombie-like atmosphere of the Monkey Run, compared to the conditions which we now enjoyed. With everyone having a totally optimistic outlook on life, it seemed more like a decade and not two-and-a-half years since those days. All those changes that had come about had really flowed from one source – my desire to host a record programme. Everything that had happened had all come about from then: the improvement of record programme presentation, the *San Fairy An* programme with new presenters and contributions from so many patients as never before; the broadcasting of sporting activities with interest from bed-ridden patients, instead of vegetating in aimless boredom; the production of a concert show never even remotely considered before and whilst I could not take any credits for all of these events, I felt contented that I had, at least, played some part, however small.

I was now 'enjoying' life, for I was now over ten stones in weight and was enjoying the good company of not only my fellow patients in the Blue Room, but also throughout the pavilion. I was active from 7.30am until 8pm (with the exception of rest hours), doing various duties and helping patients and staff. Sister had told me that I would be discharged soon, as my health and treatment were progressing well – but 'soon' in San terms could be weeks or even months! Little did I realise that my departure would be much, much sooner than I anticipated and that it would be in such bizarre circumstances that I would never have even imagined, or expected in my wildest dreams.

CHAPTER 10

An Unscheduled Departure

There were four timber chalets, each with two beds for A/D patients, situated just outside the main building, and there had always been great rivalry (and banter) between them and the main building patients. So the Musketeers decided to play a prank on them, which we had been rehearsing for a few weeks. There were rumours circulating that Italy was doing badly in the war and there was talk of a peace negotiation being done with them. So we thought of the idea to break into the BBC radio programme at 10pm and make such an announcement, broadcast to those in the chalets only. We now reckoned we were well rehearsed enough to put this across, with Moss introducing the special bulletin (as they were called in those days) and Carrigan, with his penchant for mimicry, and suitable voice, reading the startling announcement.

Just before 10pm we crept upstairs (at San pace) to the radio room, and cut off the shelter's reception from the main programme. We had just began our 'scam' when the radio room door burst open and Sister Dewar appeared. On seeing the *two* figures there (I was behind the door and unseen) she let out a loud scream and collapsed on the floor in a faint.

Whilst Moss and Carrigan were attending to Sister, I switched off the microphone and re-connected the system to the main programme again. A night nurse who had been doing her rounds on the same floor heard the commotion and came to assist Sister Dewar, who came round quite quickly. The nurse and us helped her down to the Duty Room on the ground floor where, after a glass of water, she told us she was OK. Carrigan, however, said he thought she had received such a shock that we should notify the night sister in Pavilion 2 and if necessary get another sister or staff nurse to take over Sister Dewar's duty, to which she readily agreed and then left to return to the nurses' quarters. A replacement sister did take over within about an hour and once the changeover arrangements had been completed, we returned to our room about 2am. Fortunately, few – if any – patients heard the commotion so there was no upset to them or to the night nurse.

In our room we discussed what the outcome might be. Moss said "Dismissal" but Carrigan, ever the optimist, said we could get a severe reprimand with loss of privileges for a short spell. We all dozed until about 7am then got up to follow our usual routine, as much as possible, by going for breakfast in Pavilion 2. When we got there, we knew by the glances in our direction that some news of what had happened had spread like wildfire and the 'grapevine' had worked overtime.

After breakfast, we adjourned to our room, speaking to no one, and about 9am nurse McCulloch came in (with tears in her eyes) and told us we had to report to the Duty Room at 10am *prompt*. We went to the Duty Room at exactly 10am and as we entered we saw that Matron was seated behind the desk, accompanied by Dr Baxter standing on her right and Sister standing on her left. Immediately she burst into a tirade, letting us know we had let the staff, who had cared for us so well, the patients and ourselves down and that such conduct would not be tolerated in any hospital under her supervision etc etc. She was absolutely livid and as Carrigan tried to intervene to give our reasons for such conduct, for which we wished to apologise, she told him to be quiet and not to interrupt. She seemed to go on for some time, but obviously only took two or three minutes, at the end of which she finished by saying, "You will immediately pack your belongings, and be out of the hospital by 12 noon today. Your ration book and identity card (which I still have) will be posted to your home address in two or three days. You are dismissed!" And with that she swept from the room, followed by Dr Baxter. Sister remained and gave us a nod to follow on.

As we ascended the stairs to our room, it dawned on me that we had no money; so how were we expected to get home – WALK? We had no money because for our stay in the San we never needed any money as we only needed enough to pay for our papers, magazines and church collections! We could not spend any more money as rationing was in force. So I immediately 'about turned' to go and see Sister about the arrangements for leaving. When I notified her of our problems she recognised them instantly by saying they had not thought about this. She then said to leave the matter with her and she would see what could be done. I then asked her if she could phone my employer and ask them to send word to my parents that I would be coming home that very day – I did not want to walk in on them unannounced as the shock would upset them. She agreed to do this and I gave her the telephone number.

When I got to our room, Moss was already packing his few belongings; but no Carrigan – he had some clothing in the laundry for cleaning (he was always dapper) and had gone in search of it. He returned shortly after with his garments and we all finished our packing. At the end of the rest hour, McCafferty had discretely gone to the rec and we were left with our individual thoughts until a maid came and told us to report to the Duty Room. "A reprieve?" said Carrigan, smiling. "Not damned likely," replied Moss. Before we went to the Duty Room, Don Wilson came in to inform us that he had overheard some nurses' conversation to the effect that only *two* people had been in the radio room and I could be 'in the clear'. Carrigan immediately latched on to this piece of news and to accept this version of the incident as fact, I could remain in the San. I replied that we were all in it together and my conscience would not allow me to say otherwise – did we not have a pact? "One for all and all for one!" Moss agreed it would be too dangerous to change our story at this late stage, although I did appreciate Carrigan's consideration of my position.

We then went downstairs to the Duty Room and Carrigan was invited in first. On coming out he signalled Moss to be next and when he came out I was admitted. No words had passed between us so I was not aware of what Sister had said to them (not even later) as she considered it confidential. She then said to me that she was very disappointed at the way things had turned out and whilst she appreciated that the whole episode had been a prank, which had gone drastically wrong, re-iterated the rules of the hospital regime which we were bound to observe. She then said, "I want to tell you in strict confidence and never to be mentioned anytime in the future that I wish to thank you for what you have done during your time here. This is a much happier place now, thanks to your efforts, and I hope you will continue to improve in health and that you will never forget your time here and how it has helped your recovery to a better state of health. (Until now I have observed that strict confidence!) She then gave me my expenses to get me home, saying that she had a taxi ordered for 12 noon to take us to the station (which I am sure she paid for herself!) and the remainder to pay for train tickets. I thanked her and said I would consider her expenses as a 'sub' and would send the money back as soon as possible – which I did by means of a postal order (no cheques in those days). She did not shake my hand, but simply gave me a nod, in her usual manner.

We never spoke to anyone as we stood beside our cases at the entrance (or should that be exit) hall, until the taxi came at about 11.45am. We boarded the taxi with our cases, with Carrigan sitting in front with the driver and Moss and I behind. As the taxi was about to leave, Carrigan said to the driver, "Drive slowly past Pavilions 1 and 2 as we leave Pavilion 3, until we get to the main gates." Moss looked at me with a quizzical look – why? Then we realised that as we drove along, almost every patient who was entitled to be up and there was out, waving us goodbye. Carrigan was milking the situation to the limit – we felt like royalty! Lunches were late being served that day!

CHAPTER 11

Separate Ways

As we passed through the hospital gates, the taxi picked up speed and when we got to the station, as we got out, in our haste we forgot to tip the driver. We entered the station, went to the booking office, bought third class tickets for Glasgow and then sat in the waiting room for the arrival of the train. We were now leaving behind our Shangri-la existence and re-entering the real world – although we hoped we would not age as quickly as the characters in the novel of that title! When the train arrived, we were startled by the noise, which seemed to be exaggerated after the peace and tranquillity we had enjoyed for two or three years amongst the Renfrewshire hills. There was little conversation as we placed our cases on the racks and even during the journey as we each had our own thoughts, until Carrigan suddenly said, "What are those things in that field?"

Moss and I both looked but could not see anything but sheep, and Moss said, "There's nothing there but sheep."

Carrigan replied, "Of course, I didn't recognise them as I haven't seen any farm animals for years and wondered what they were."

It was good to know he had not lost his zany sense of

humour! He then re-iterated his opinion that I should have stayed out of the Duty Room inquisition, but I again reminded him that we had a pact: "One for all and all for one," the last time such a phrase was ever used!

We said farewell at the shell, the main focus point known to all Glaswegians in the main concourse of the central station in the usual manner by shaking hands, wishing "good health" and hoping we may meet again. The Three Musketeers were then disbanded! We each faced an uncertain future health-wise as we had never received any documentation to confirm our present state of health. We then went our separate ways: Carrigan to his tram to Maryhill, Moss to board his bus for Rutherglen and me to get my train to Hamilton. I never saw Carrigan again, but I visited Moss some two years later, only to find him in very poor health, and indeed, he passed away shortly after my visit.

I noticed from the destination board that I had some time to wait for my train, so I ventured into Renfield Street, but the noise of the clanging of trams, the roar of buses and lorries and the clatter of the Clydesdale horses hooves on the cobbled streets seemed to assail my ear drums and were such that I hastily sought the sanctuary of the station concourse. However, I did see something which I had never seen for about three years – I actually saw people *running* for buses and trams! Actually *running*! They obviously had never heard of San pace! It certainly looked like another world from the one I had just left – I hoped I would soon get used to all that hustle and bustle! I caught my train to Hamilton, but when I went to get the local bus, I discovered that the bus stop had been changed to a different location. But I did board the bus tendering what had been the fare I had paid three years previously, hoping that inflation had not struck during my absence!

I got off the bus and crossed the road to enter the close leading to our house – situated above our shop that my parents had sold as there was no family to operate the business. As I climbed the stairs, I began to go slightly weak at the knees, for I well knew the sort of reception I would receive – and it would not be of the "welcome home" type. I also hoped Sister had managed to carry out my request to get a message to my parents via my employer.

When I entered the house, my parents were waiting for me (to quote Burns "nursing their wrath to keep it warm"), and after a disdainful look from both, Father launched into a tirade of criticism of how stupid I had been and how I had let everyone down who had helped me in the four years since I had been diagnosed. I was 21 years old and in all those years never once had I seen Father angry (never mind in a tantrum!) He was a gentle man (gentleman!) who suffered from pneumomycosis, having worked in the Lanarkshire coalfields as a miner for some 50 years. He had often related the conditions of working in coal seams to me – with as little as 3ft headroom in 2-3in of water that had seeped through from the rivers Clyde and Avon, with only a flickering of light from a carbide lamp. I was filled with remorse, and as I thought he was going to faint, placed my hand on his shoulder, which he gently eased away. Mother then continued the condemnation in similar vein, at the end of which I could only humbly plead how sorry I was for all the trouble I had caused. The weather outside was fine and dry, but the atmosphere in the house was distinctly chilly and continued thus for two or three days.

CHAPTER 12

Alternative Treatment

The following day I went to see Dr Gilmour, but had to wait a further two days before seeing him as I would need him to arrange further 'refills' for my continued treatment. When I did see him, I was treated to the same reception as I had received at home as he too was disappointed in my conduct. However, he said to return in a few days' time, when he hoped to be able to make suitable arrangements for treatment, probably in Glasgow. Two days later he told me I had to go to Black Street clinic in Glasgow and gave me a note to take with me. When I asked him about returning to work, he replied that this would depend on the clinic's findings. When I arrived at Black Street, the doctor informed me that no treatment was required for another two weeks. When I asked him about returning to work, he said he had no objection, providing I did not work full-time, and gave me a note to that effect to take back to Dr Gilmour.

On returning to Dr Gilmour, we concurred with the decision, and said that if my employer was willing to re-engage me at the previous hours of 10am to 4pm, he would be happy with that arrangement, although I should still avoid all crowded places as before. When I saw my employers, they were only too happy to re-instate me, as there was a shortage of staff because of war conditions. My re-instatement was for the same hours (but with no increase in salary) – but I was quite happy to return. The staff personnel had obviously changed during my time 'on leave' and I now found myself in a supervising capacity with greater responsibility.

On my next visit to Black Street for treatment, I discovered that this was also the main clinic for patients with venereal diseases in the Glasgow area (and I thought I was bad enough with TB!) I did not wish to be infected with their particular ailment and whilst waiting for our respective treatments, we kept a few yards apart! However, after a further few visits, I was told my treatment was now completed and no further visits were contemplated, although I should check with my own doctor on a regular basis.

I then went back to my old routine of Monday to Friday at the office and on Saturdays and Sundays walking along all the quiet roads around the Hamilton area, in all kinds of weather. As my pals, who were not in the forces, were working long hours, including Sundays, they spent their spare time going to football, cinema or dancing, all of which were still banned to me. I became a loner – yet again.

After just over a year of this monotonous routine, with no highs or lows, I awoke one Sunday with an unusual taste in my mouth – I knew instantly what it was! It was the taste of blood! And from my experience with other patients who had suffered this, I knew I was haemorrhaging from my lung. First thought – DON'T PANIC – and whatever you do – DON'T COUGH! I called Mother to bring me a bowl into which I could expectorate and told her to ask my sister to go immediately to see our GP Dr Coutts, who I knew would likely be available at his home as he was a Jew and certainly not attending church! I had never spoken sharply to my sister before, but being rather upset at the current situation I was now in, told her to hurry up. This set her scurrying on her way as time was of the essence. We had no telephone, and the nearest telephone kiosk was almost as far away as the doctor's house, hence the reason to visit him. Second thought – what if it was the other lung that was haemorrhaging? If such was the case, and both lungs were affected, then I should prepare myself for the arrival of the Great Reaper, who, with one swing of his scythe, would cut the brittle thread of life.

I continued to haemorrhage! As I looked at my parents, I realised the further anguish they now suffered. I saw the disappointment in their eyes, for it was now four years since being told I had TB and now I was back to square one – in fact I was now worse off than before because I had never haemorrhaged in all that time. I looked at Mother, who steadfastly, every Saturday, for all my time in the San, had left home at about 10am and returned at about 7pm in order to visit me in summer's heat and winter's cold, and who, never once, made any word of complaint. As I observed more closely, they seemed to have aged considerably beyond their years – and all because of me!

I continued to haemorrhage! Final thought: as I watched them, I thought maybe I was a little hasty in my decision to call the doctor – perhaps it may have been better to let nature take its course and literally let life ebb away. It would be painful for them, and I knew they would grieve, but at least I would not be committing them to a further four years (or possibly even more) of uncertainty. They did not deserve such treatment. What right had I to condemn them to such a situation? I continued to haemorrhage, but less frequently!

I had reached the nadir of my whole life and in my present state of mind decided that if there was no marked improvement in my condition, I would simply succumb. It may have seemed the coward's way out, but for my family's sake and my peace of mind, my sacrifice would be well worth it. As my sister left, I told her to ask Dr Coutts to bring calcium, which I knew from my experience in the San would stem the blood flow. After what seemed an eternity, but was actually only about 20 minutes, the doctor and sister arrived. When I asked him about an injection of calcium, he said that in haste he had not brought any with him. He left immediately, returning shortly to give me a good dose, which, fortunately, activated quickly. By mid-afternoon my sputum showed only a speck of blood and this had cleared completely by evening.

Until now my thoughts had all been negative, so what had happened to positive thinking? Were things really as bad as I imagined? I recalled Jim Russell's remarks these few years ago: "Go for it, Jack, you can do it!" I remembered the Musketeers' daily chant: "Every day in every way I'm getting better," and "Live for today for tomorrow may be even better." Perhaps, after all, there might be something in this 'positive thinking' lark. Try it, you've nothing to lose – but your life!

On the Monday, unknown to me, Dr Coutts had been in touch with Dr Gilmour, who, in turn, had contacted Hairmyres Hospital, which resulted in a visit to the hospital on the Thursday. I was seen by a doctor who introduced himself as Professor Bruce Dick. He thoroughly examined me without my parents being present and advised me that since AP treatment had already been performed and it could not be re-activated as my lung was now adhered to my plural cavity wall, the only action to be taken would be a major operation called thorocoplasty. My immediate reaction was "NO WAY" as I had seen two patients go from the San to the Royal Infirmary in Glasgow to undergo such an operation, neither of whom fully recovered, leaving them semi-invalids in their 20s and 30s.

The operation, at that time, had a 50/50 chance of complete success and even if you survived the five or six hour surgery, you were disfigured for life, having to wear a specially-made surgical jacket to protect the upper body from any knocks. The professor assured me that I was a suitable patient for this operation (he would!) and discussed with my parents the procedure. After this, as he was leaving, with a flick of his stethoscope (his characteristic style), he said, "I'll see you in Hairmyres in three weeks' time," to which my reply was the same as previously: "NO WAY."

That evening I discussed the matter fully with my parents, explaining the operation from the patient's point of view and detailing the likelihood of success, as I saw it. Father, in his quiet yet firm manner, said he had great faith in the medical profession and taking into consideration all they had done for me in the past, I must put my faith in them as he was prepared to do. Mother and Sister readily concurred with that view. Even although I did not agree with their decision, as this was their unanimous choice, I decided to accept it as I did not wish to cause any dissent. After all, they were my family! I wonder what Mr Hobson's choice would have been?

A few days later, I received a letter from Hairmyres hospital advising me to report there on a certain Monday at 9am. On receiving this letter, I wrote to Highet, who was now home, telling him of my position and he replied that he would visit me in hospital on the Wednesday immediately following my admission. He had been a very good friend (and still is!) and I looked forward to his visit, which I knew would cheer me up.

Three weeks later, on the prescribed Monday at 9am I entered Hairmyres hospital and was admitted to an eight-bed ward on the first floor in their TB unit and allocated the third bed on the left. I noticed as I entered that the first bed on the right was occupied by a patient who was propped up and surrounded by a number of pillows and who, I observed, seemed to be gasping for breath even more than I had experienced at my induction to AP. At about lunch time I went over to see him and introduced myself. He informed me that he had undergone the same operation that was about to be performed on me. If my introduction to the San was disheartening, then this was even more so, for as I looked at him I got a reflection of myself, in a similar state, a few days hence. I had experienced disappointment before, but this seemed too much to bear – its a sobering thought to see yourself as others see you and not a pretty sight! The cure seemed much worse than the disease, but there was no turning back – the die was cast!

On the Tuesday morning the entourage – consisting of the professor, house doctor, sister and staff nurse – entered the ward and as he approached my bed, the professor said, "This afternoon you will have a series of tomographs taken," and with a flick of his stethoscope added, "I'll do you on Friday." I did not like his tone of voice: 'I'll do you' seemed to be just a little too ominous!

In the afternoon I went to the X-ray department for my tomographs and when I came back, a nurse entered with two bottles of dark liquid, one of which she gave to my friend in the corner bed and the other she placed on top of my locker. On examining the label on the bottle, it said 'Mackeson Stout'. I asked the nurse why, to which she replied, "You have to take this every day until further notice." We were the only ones to get a bottle in the whole ward! We must have been real invalids in much need of a tonic! I called the nurse to say that I couldn't open the bottle, so she went away and returned with (would you believe?) a bottle opener.

I had heard the old slogan "An apple a day keeps the doctor

away" which I immediately changed to say "A Mackeson a day keeps the surgeon away" Some hope! I did not take my tonic, but kept it for Highet's visit. Can you imagine stout being prescribed today, under the NHS? Bring back the Matron, I say!

On the Wednesday, Highet kept his promise and visited as agreed. To 'celebrate' the occasion, we each drank our 'tonic' and spent the whole visiting time reminiscing about our San days. All too soon it was time for him to leave. As he prepared to leave, we shook hands, he wished me good luck and said, "See you in about a week's time – don't be late!" He was more optimistic than I at that time.

Late on Thursday afternoon (after my tonic) I was being prepared for surgery the following day and was shaved all over my chest and armpits, then painted with iodine. I was then dressed in a loose-fitting theatre gown and there followed the customary enema. As I settled down for the night, my nerves overcame me and I started to shake all over, for I knew the stark choice which lay ahead on the morrow – a 50/50 chance of coming through the operation, and if successful, a life ahead of being a semi-invalid.

Or could there yet be another alternative? Being unable to sleep, I asked the night nurse for a sleeping pill and, unexpectedly, she gave me one. In the morning when I awoke, I felt completely relaxed and was 'serenity personified' as I now accepted that fate would have its say. My mood, however, immediately changed to one of impatience, for I now wanted the 'evil deed' over, once and for all, irrespective of the outcome. The die had been cast, and could not be reclaimed!

CHAPTER 13

A Miracle Cure

I looked at my watch. The time was just after 8am but time seemed to have stopped – it seemed to pass more slowly as my impatience increased. Where were the medical team? Come on! Let's get on with the job in hand! The second-hand on my watch hardly moved and the minute hand seemed completely static. Come on, you surgical team, show face!

At about 9am, after what seemed like the longest hour of my life, the entourage entered the ward and as he approached my bed, the professor flipped his stethoscope, saying, "I'll see you in the Duty Room." This looked like the final briefing before the action would begin. As was the accepted custom, I waited until the group had left the ward then put on my dressing gown and slippers and with steps even slower than San pace approached the Duty Room door and tapped quietly. "Come," came the voice from within.

As I entered the room, I saw that the group were studying a series of X-rays on a battery of monitors and I immediately thought that the professor may have called me to tell me that my other lung was affected, and I blurted out, "Is my other lung affected?"

A short pause, then: "Don't be silly boy."

I was almost 23 years old. Was this a compliment on my youthful appearance? I doubted that very much! A slightly longer pause, then a question that took me by surprise – "Have you ever heard of or read a book entitled *The Walking Miracle*?"

"Yes."

A further long pause, then, "Briefly describe it to me."

(This book was the most read book in the San library and everyone who read it hoped their outcome would be the same as the author.)

I then told him the book had been written in the 30s by a man who had been a patient in a Swiss sanatorium for about three years and who had haemorrhaged two or three times and after his latest haemorrhage had been examined by the doctors there only to find there was no trace of TB to be seen. X-rays were taken to confirm this. The patient was then discharged and lived a healthy life for several years thereafter. They could find no medical, or indeed, any rational explanation for this happening and the whole episode became the subject of much discussion and debate in medical circles worldwide.

There then followed a long, long, pause. "THAT is what happened to you," the professor said. I collapsed into the chair, for I did not know whether to laugh or cry – I was completely stunned! However, I faintly heard him say, "I will keep you in over the weekend for observation, and on Monday you will be X-rayed again and if the position remains status-quo, you can be discharged on Tuesday morning."

I returned to the ward, although I did not remember doing so and much to the amazement of my fellow patients, dressed myself in ordinary clothes. I did not divulge what had taken place in the Duty Room. However, I swear to this very day, that I levitated all the way from the ward to the day room at the far end of the corridor where I sat for quite some time, unaware of what was happening around me, as my mind seemed to have gone completely blank. A walking miracle? Impossible! In the afternoon I did *not* receive my bottle of Mackeson stout! Mother and Father (who despite being in very poor health) had been determined to visit me after my operation and were due to visit me that evening so I went to the hospital's main entrance on the ground floor to meet and greet them.

I will never forget the sight of the amazement on their faces when they saw me standing there, all in one piece and large as life! I quickly explained what had happened and we all fell into one big embrace with tears of joy and relief, but for me the tears were more for my parents who had supported me so faithfully for four long years. I told Mother not to visit me over the weekend – but you know what mothers are like – she visited me on Saturday, Sunday and Monday!

On the Monday, I went for an X-ray and on the Tuesday morning was called to the Duty Room where the professor told me I was being discharged but that he would like me to come back for his master class, which he held for student doctors and for which I would receive a fee – my bus fares! His parting words to me were, "Don't volunteer for the forces, or you may be accepted! Good luck and continued good health!"

About three weeks later, I received a letter from him asking me to attend his master class. When I reported to his consulting room, I met four or five trainee doctors, who were asked by the professor to examine "this young man". (I had gone from being a boy to being a young man in the course of a few weeks!) Naturally they were unable to ascertain for sure what my case really was, as their stethoscopes could not pick up any traces of TB. I could see by the puzzled expressions on their faces that they were unsure what to say until one rather timorously suggested that I may have suffered from TB as he was aware that the professor was an acknowledged expert in that field. "Correct," said the professor, and then explained my case from original diagnosis to the present time and added rather proudly (I thought), "You are witnessing a phenomenon which you may never encounter again in your careers – but keep this in mind for the future." (I had gone from boy to young man to phenomenon – that really was progress!) We then shook hands all round and I left the consulting room. I was never recalled for any further master classes.

Old medical saying: "Doctors may treat – but nature heals."

The war was now almost over and those in the forces, who had fought for King and Country would be returning with more experience of life (and death!) and probably increased skills, ready to face a new world order!

Those who had set off some six years ago, intent, hopefully, of surviving the conflict, and had done so, would now expect to reap the benefits for their efforts, by being rewarded with the promise of better employment prospects, better housing, improved health prospects and a better standard of life than before – and rightly so!

I, too, had set out in 1940 to survive the conflict like them, but FATE had decreed we take entirely different and diverse routes to reach our present situation. So what did the future hold for me, whose contribution to the war effort had been NIL? I had very little opportunity to extend my experience of life, having been institutionalised in a regime where rest and relaxation had been the order of the day and where severe, extended bouts of lassitude caused a lack of desire or interest to further any skills necessary to face an uncertain future.

I still lived in dread of being asked the pointed question: "What did *you* do during the war?" By some miracle I was still alive and in reasonably good health, but how would I fare in the immediate post war years, and hopefully beyond?

That, however, is another story.

EPILOGUE

Some 60 years later, my thoughts occasionally stray to that inexplicable event which happened on that particular/special Friday morning, when a prominent member of the medical profession in Scotland told me that I was a walking miracle. It set me thinking: In addition to the gentleman in the Swiss sanatorium and myself, are there any other recorded instances of walking miracles?

ADDENDUM

A few years later, I was standing watching the various organisations assemble for their annual march to church for Remembrance Day. The parade was headed by the Royal British Legion with their members proudly displaying their ribbons and medals deservedly earned for their services in the various war zones in which they had participated in the six years of the war. In their ranks, I noticed many that I knew before the war with whom I had been acquainted at sporting events. I did not, however, see any previously close friends from my school days and early employment – for they had all made the ultimate sacrifice.

Wee Harry, who had just beaten me to be dux at primary school, had been killed on the beaches at Dunkirk. Billy, who had been a navigator in the RAF, had been killed when his plane was shot down over Germany in the last flight of his tour of duties before being posted to a ground-based position in southern England. Joe, who had been captain of our school football team and who had great potential to make his way in that sport, had been a member of the parachute regiment and had been killed at Arnhem. Adam, who had been in the RAF as a heavy goods driver and had survived the conflict, but caught a disease whilst on operations in Europe immediately after VE day, only to die of his illness a short time after returning home. I missed them all greatly.

As the parade moved off, behind their RBL banner, I

realised they were all members of an exclusive organisation – in this respect I did not have the necessary qualifications to join their ranks as I had not served in the forces. I was still an outsider looking in.

The organisation was formed, quite rightly, to look after their interests and to provide help and assistance should it be required. This concept was never more fully exemplified than in the displays on television for many years, at the Cenotaph and the Royal Albert Hall, where every facet of British life was shown for all to admire – and yet no word was made of the society of which I was a member – the T.B. brigade!

To be an active member of our society, all you need is a persistently hacking cough and a germ laden spit, preferably with a streak of blood through it! We don't have any recruitment drives – because we don't want anyone to join us! We are, to some extent, a secret society, (no, not the masons, with fancy hand shakes or funny signs!) because we don't know (unless by chance) who our members are, or how many of us there are – we keep quiet about our membership!

We have no headquarters anywhere, no branch offices, no regular meetings, no advertising slogans, no poppy days, no fundraising activities – yet we survive – just! We were the lepers of the 19th and 20th centuries and whilst our membership does sometimes decline, we are gaining new members every day. Our recruiting grounds are not only the affluent parts of western society, but especially the under-developed third world nations, in a swathe from South America through Africa, Eastern Europe, the Middle East, the Asian sub-continent, Eastern Asia and Russia, where facilities to combat our 'recruitment' are very poor, or even non-existent.

But who (WHO even) are doing anything about it? Over the years, various summit meetings have been convened with a view to review eradication of this horrible disease, but no, or very little, impact has been made to 'Make TB History'. It will take much in the way of money and resources, but what is really needed is a will and determination by all world leaders to actually tackle the problem head-on and in so doing save thousands of lives. The irony is that we are all potential 'recruits' for we all have the tubercle gene in our bodies. Even as an 'ex-member' I could again become an active member – all I need to do is allow my immune system to run down, by catching a virus and by neglecting to lead a healthy life. So eating healthy food, regular exercise by walking five miles in reasonably good weather, with regular rest periods can all help to keep TB at bay. If, however, you should be unfortunate enough to join our ranks you will, at least, have the satisfaction of knowing that with the enormous advances made by science and technology, you will not need to undergo the primitive methods of 60 years ago in order to achieve a quick recuperation period and restoration to good health. But spare a thought for those members in our ranks who are not so fortunate to have the facilities which we in the west enjoy and who do not even have the 'luxury' of a cool, clear glass of water! Sixty years ago I did have such a 'luxury' during a very severe spell of really harsh winter conditions when, on one occasion, the water in my glass on the cabinet at the side of my bed was frozen solid! Fortunately, in recent years, TB is quite rare in the UK so being affected seems an unlikely prospect, but with the nearly epidemic figures now showing up in Africa, we must continue to be on guard.

When I had come out of the San and returned to work on a part-time basis, a very interesting incident happened. One day, Mother was standing at the local bus stop when she was approached by a woman who asked the following question: "Why is your son not in the forces like my son, and does not seem to do any real work?" Mother looked her straight in the eye (at which she was very good!) and replied, "My son would be only too happy to exchange places with your son, but I doubt if your son would change places with him – you see, my son has TB!" On hearing that, the other woman involuntarily took a step back. This incident amply illustrates the attitude of some people at that time to the stigma of TB. When Mother told me the story, she laughed heartily, saying, "And I didn't even have TB!"

Among all the plethora of words written recently about the threat of terrorism, the following quotation seems particularly appropriate: "Terrorism isn't about bombs and bullets. Its about fear and panic in our hearts and minds." In some parts of the world, as mentioned previously, TB is still rampant, which is why children whose parents and grandparents also come from these countries are still most vulnerable. Is the risk of spreading this disease not still real? TB can be passed on by droplets if you are about a mile away from a 'spitter'. It can also be spread by finer particles that hang in the air, lingering in a crowded place, especially transport and theatres etc.

Know Thy Neighbour was a programme that we broadcast on San radio some 60 years ago, but as you sit on a crowded bus or train, or travel by air to some of the more exquisite holiday resorts in the swathe of our 'recruiting' areas, do you, then, know your neighbour? Does he/she have a bad cough, or did he/she clear the phlegm from their throat before or after leaving the vehicle? Warnings are given about being alert to any suspicions of terrorism, but could your travelling companion show any signs of being a 'dreaded terrorist' or could he/she be just as deadly? In our radio programme, we, at least, knew our contributor had TB but what about your immediate neighbour? He/she does not look any different from ourselves, do they? And yet, they may be a silent threat, if not quite a terrorist. Over the years (and probably in the not too distant future) TB has killed more people than all the known terrorist organisations put together.

So does TB have a more latent, and perhaps threatening, undercurrent? We may not be terrorists, but we do pose an ever-present menace and a serious threat to all humanity, and with every natural catastrophe, such as tsunamis and hurricanes, the 'silent enemy' is still with us. The cost of the war against terrorism and Al Queida may be massive but let us never forget that resources can, and should be, made available so that I may yet live to see TB made history.

I am ever grateful to the Three Musketeers for initiating me into their interpretation of 'positive thinking' all those years ago. At that time, after a few months of sheer misery, my outlook on life was pretty pessimistic, but they changed all that. Like them, I became a super-optimist. Their daily mantra still echoes, although now there is but one frail and weak voice – every day and in every way, I'm getting better!

I am now 85 years old and fully intend to live to be 100 – or die in the attempt!